THE SPLITS

How to help your kids navigate separation and divorce

Bron O'Loan

'For those experiencing one of the most difficult and traumatic times in their lives, the best guidance they can receive is not only clear and practical, but also pragmatic. This book ticks all of those boxes, and does so in spades.'

Jerome Doraisamy, deputy editor, *Lawyers Weekly*

'Groundbreaking and long overdue. *The Splits* provides separating parents with accurate knowledge to maximise their children's emotions and futures at this highly vulnerable time. Fear is replaced with understanding. Bron O'Loan's professional and lived experience has created a very readable guide to understanding Family Law. This at a time in our lives when empathy, connection and effective communication is paramount. A MUST HAVE for all parents, grandparents, families and professionals.'

Sue Hawkins, Therapist and Senior Clinician

'The first and most obvious element of Bron O'Loan's wonderful new book is that she clearly cares. Her compassion, kindness and playful nature can seem a little at odds on a topic that is so often filled with difficulty and harshness, but it really works. I have great admiration for the book that Bron has written, one that will help parents be the best version of themselves when traversing separation.'

Andrew Griffiths, International Bestselling Author

'Managing the challenges that separation and divorce throw our way is hard enough, but then finding the courage to support your children too takes something else altogether. Bron's wise, careful and kind advice is invaluable for all parents trying to navigate this difficult time and will empower you to support your children in the best way possible.'

Clarissa Rayward, Director, Accredited Family Law Specialist, Collaborative Lawyer and Mediator

'*The Splits* tackles some of the most uncomfortable conversations parents can have with their children and acknowledges that children have very different perspectives on things. Bron has done a terrific job with providing parents with useful tips and explains the range of experiences that kids are likely to be experiencing. Bron uses her experience from talking to kids about what they need and presents it in a compelling way that will allow parents to be able to support their kids. Well done Bron, definitely a must read for parents navigating a breakup.'

Gloria Larman, Chief Executive Officer, Women's Justice Network

'*The Splits* offers parents helpful tips, strategies, and insight into how to best support their children during an often difficult time of separation. Bron engages her readers by using her natural style with light humour, while discussing the most important and serious issues for kids with parents who are separating. This book really is a must read for any parent wanting the best outcome for their children.'

Louise Hethorn, Principal, Your Property Lawyers Pty Ltd

'Of all the books to have in your "divorcing with kids" survival kit, this one would have to be top of your list. A practical and easily digestible guide to what to do and what NOT to do, this book is a "must have" for any parent who wishes to provide their children with safe passage through separation.'

Anna Marshall, Director, People Mastery Pty Ltd

'A frank, fearless and fabulous guide for parents who want the best for their children as they navigate the tricky waters through separation. A successful family lawyer who has supported hundreds of families in their separation journey, Bron's compassion, wisdom and gentle humour shine through on every page. A must read if you want to help your children thrive as they transition to living in two homes.'

Julia Brierley, Principal, Sydney Dispute Resolution Pty Ltd

'I found Bron O'Loan's book *The Splits* a very easy to read book, packed with accurate and relevant information about the topic. As a psychologist dealing with relationship breakdowns over the past 25 years, it is refreshing to read a book that can be so helpful in the detail of issues arising for parents and their children when faced with divorce.'

Lorraine Corne, Consulting Psychologist and Author

'As all of us know, separation and divorce can be especially hard for children. Often unintended, they struggle with the world they knew so well changing rapidly and schools are often called on to support families in these circumstances. Bron's practical, but pastoral guide will assist any parent seeking to understand how best to support their children through this experience so that their wellbeing is prioritised.'

Mark Tannock, Principal St Aloysius' College

'Bron's expertise as a family law practitioner, together with her life experience and insight as a mum, teacher and business owner, make this text an absolute treasure chest of gems on navigating one of the most emotional and stressful experiences that life presents - separation, kids and divorce. Highly recommend for anyone on the separation journey.'

Laura Gardiner, Senior Solicitor, Legal Aid, Family Law Litigation Division, Legal Aid NSW

ABOUT BRON O'LOAN

Bron O'Loan is a passionate Divorce lawyer practising in Sydney, Australia as the Director of the boutique family law firm, O'Loan Family Law.

With an enthusiasm for helping people, Bron's core focus is to guide her clients to get through the splits with their family relationships intact enough to ensure the kids are okay.

As well as her fancy lawyer job, Bron is a mum to three hungry, and often moody, teenagers, an avid writer and an ardent advocate of supporting domestic and family violence victims.

Bron wasn't always a family lawyer. In fact, upon leaving school, Bron loved the experience so much she became a primary school teacher. Since then, she has gone on to sell newspaper advertising, travelled around Australia and the world as a product manager and trainer for a large IT firm, was the author of a Masters' Degree program for teachers, was a lecturer at Charles Sturt University and ran a successful online retail store.

In 2012 Bron commenced her journey into law as a mature age student and held fast to her view that empathy is the key and hugging clients is often necessary. In 2016 Bron decided that a bit more study would do the trick and obtained a Masters in Family Law where she continued to hone her skills as a family lawyer.

After many years working under the tutelage of two very different but equally fierce and supportive family law mentors, and in the midst of a global pandemic, Bron founded O'Loan Family Law. She now manages a highly effective and intrepid team of likeminded legal eagles, who help to guide separating couples in reaching an amicable settlement.

Known for her ability to inspire, energise and collaborate, Bron is a well-respected member of the legal community. Upon meeting Bron or reading her book, you will come away from the experience ready to take action and make positive changes to get yourself and your kids through the separation journey.

You can contact Bron at her practice, O'Loan Family Law Pty Ltd:

Phone: (+61) 2 9922 2230
Email: bron@oloanfamilylaw.com.au
Web: www.bronoloan.com
www.oloanfamilylaw.com.au

or at hello@bronoloan.com.

ACKNOWLEDGEMENTS

Like many before me, I have always wanted to write a book. But actually committing to it and telling the first person that it's on like Donkey Kong wasn't just about me taking that step. Starting out on this journey, it quickly became apparent to me that although I held the role of the keyboard warrior, spending countless hours crafting the sentences in this book, there were so many others involved in the process.

To begin, I'm not sure I would ever have had the conviction or resolve to do this without the initial gentle shove from my amazing colleagues. The support from the happiest group of lawyers I have ever met has been heartwarming and humbling and I am constantly grateful for your friendship.

To my book writing buddy, Anna Marshall, your infectious smile and continuous positivity helped me to get through the inevitable roadblocks that we face on the writing journey. Thank you for keeping it real.

Michael, Anna and the supportive team at Publish Central, your dedication to creating a quality product has been very much appreciated and even though we did the rounds on the cover design, we ended up back at the beginning with the very first design which still makes me smile. You guys certainly know what you're doing.

A big thank you to a man with some serious heart, Andrew Griffiths. Thank you for all your guidance and mentorship. You are an absolute inspiration and have my deepest respect. My world is definitely a better place for having met you.

To my clients, past and present, I could not have written this book without you. Your stories, your journeys and your truth have been an inspiration and I am forever grateful that you chose to trust in me to walk with you on your path to separation. Thank you.

Finn, Tara and Grace, you are the loves of my life and the reason I reach for the stars every day. Thank you for being my biggest supporters and for understanding and accepting that success comes with hard work and dedication. I see those traits in each of you and you make me so proud.

And finally, to Greg. Without you I would not have been able to do this thing. Your sacrifices, your unlimited support and belief in me is of legendary status. You have given me the gift of time and afforded me a deep respect that all women have the right to experience. And for that I am so grateful.

For Greg, Finn, Tara and Grace,
y'all are my why.

One day Alice came to a fork in the road
and saw a Cheshire cat in a tree.

'Which road do I take?' she asked.

'Where do you want to go?' was his response.

'I don't know,' Alice answered.

'Then,' said the cat, 'it doesn't matter.'

' – so long as I get somewhere,'
Alice added as an explanation.

Lewis Carroll, *Alice's Adventures in Wonderland*

First published in 2021 by Bron O'Loan
bron@oloanfamilylaw.com.au
www.bronoloan.com
www.oloanfamilylaw.com.au

A catalogue entry for this book is available from the National Library of Australia.

ISBN: 978-1-922553-39-3

Printed in Australia by McPherson's Printing
Project management and text design by Publish Central
Cover design by Peter Reardon

Cover image and images on pages 173, 189, 229, 232 © Shutterstock.
Images on pages 7, 53, 91, 153 © iStock.

The paper this book is printed on is certified as environmentally friendly.

CONTENTS

Introduction
KIDS KNOW STUFF

In my time working as a primary school teacher, and then as a family lawyer and an Independent Children's Lawyer, I've spent countless hours with all types of kids – young and old, shy and outgoing, friendly and not so friendly. When I think back on my interactions with those kids, there is one thing they all have in common. One central theme that permeates every kid's humanness.

Curiosity.

They listen, they watch, they are sponges. Kids know stuff. Sometimes they know more than we realise. You know it's true.

It's a trait every kid has. They are naturally curious. They want to know things. They ask questions. They are little inquisitors with a passion to get to an answer.

HOW DO YOU PREPARE YOUR KIDS FOR YOUR SEPARATION?

So what happens if you find yourself going through the splits? And I'm guessing you've either already arrived in Splitsville or you're planning to travel there in the not-so-distant future. Otherwise, and let's be frank, you wouldn't have picked up this book.

How do you prepare your kids for this separation journey, and how do you talk to them about it? How do you satisfy your children's natural curiosity to find out what's going on?

If you *are* going through the splits, your kids are involved whether you like it or not. It's inevitable that you're going to have to have some conversations with the kids about the situation. But where do you draw the line between explaining what is going on and oversharing?

Having conversations with your kids about your separation is important. But it's equally important to understand that some conversations should be left out.

What do I mean?

Well, imagine your 14-year-old daughter coming to you and asking, 'Why are you and Dad in court?' And imagine that same daughter also asking, 'Does this mean that I'm going to have to speak to a judge?'

How would you respond to such questions?

MOVING FORWARD

There's often a part of us that wants to blame the other parent for starting the separation process or for being in court. It might be that it actually *is* your ex's fault because they started the court proceedings. But does it really help your kids to know that? Is that the kind of information that is going to make their separation journey easier?

You'd have to agree with me when I say that blaming your ex is probably not going to help the situation.

We as parents are hardwired to reach out and make everything okay for our kids. But sometimes, if we are struggling with our own emotions, we can find ourselves responding to our children in inappropriate ways.

Also, and perhaps even more concerning for us, we may not actually have all the answers for our kids. How could we?

Having worked as a family lawyer for many years, I have encountered lots of mums and dads who are deeply concerned about what they should and shouldn't be sharing with their kids about their separation. That kind of worry has the capacity to keep you up at night. And you need your sleep more than ever right now.

EVERY SEPARATION JOURNEY IS UNIQUE

If you've found yourself in the depths of your very own separation journey, take some time to find out how this might impact your kids. Do some research. Invest some time into reading this book. Talk to your family lawyer and ask questions. Don't be shy to ask for help and advice about how you should be updating your kids at each stage of your separation. And how you should be talking to your kids about the future.

But wait. Is that you I hear saying, 'Well, Bron, that's all good and well, but I wouldn't even know where to start with talking to my kids about our family separation'?

I'm a mum to three hungry teenagers. I've also worked as a primary school teacher and then as a family lawyer and an Independent Children's Lawyer. In all of my experiences with kids (and there have been hundreds of thousands of hours of me having conversations with kids in my work and in my home life), I've had the opportunity to practise speaking with kids and to work out how to talk to them about important stuff.

Now by no means am I suggesting that I know exactly how *your* kids are going to react to your separation. How could I? I haven't met you, or them. We haven't had the benefit of an in-depth discussion about what your kids are like, what makes each of them tick and what your unique separation journey looks like. But I can draw on my experiences to give you a roadmap for getting your kids through this difficult phase of their lives and to help them find their separation story.

There are definitely dos and don'ts that you should be aware of. And from my experience, knowing how your kids will react to receiving certain types of information can absolutely be impacted by their age, maturity levels and how they are mentally and emotionally tracking. You are the best person to know this about your kids. You are the expert here. But like all experts, you will benefit from a roadmap to keep you focused on what's really important for your kids *right now*.

This book will show you how to navigate the journey and watch for and interpret signs from your kids. This will help you to make sure you know when and how to have the important conversations you need to have with your kids about separation. But it goes further than that. You don't want to just know about *what* to say to your kids, but *how* to say it, *when* to say it, *what* to ask them, *how* to check in with them, and *how* to support them moving forward. You want to know how to future proof your kids.

This book is for parents who want to support their kids going through separation and divorce. It's a guide for what you should be talking about with your children and, just as importantly, what you should be leaving out of the conversation.

HOW TO GET THE MOST OUT OF THIS BOOK

I've written this book to guide you through the conversations you need to have with your kids about separation and divorce. It's a book worth reading if you are a parent or a carer who really cares about how your family separation is going to impact the children - because let's face it, your separation will impact them. A lot.

I want you to be armed with the useful information that you are going to need to get through your separation journey, with a goal of ensuring your kids come out of the journey better for it. This book will give you the confidence to support your kids during your separation, giving you the right information to help them understand what's going on, what their involvement will be, and that ultimately it will all be okay, so that you can understand and make decisions about the bigger picture: the future life of your kids and you.

I suggest you read this book a bit like you would read a map. You don't necessarily need to study the whole thing at once, just the parts that are relevant to your journey. Don't set out to read it all in one sitting. Rather, take your time and dip in and out of it as you need it.

Use the parts and chapters to work out what bits you need now and what bits you might need down the track. For example, if you're not in court with your ex, you might skip the section called 'A conversation about the legal system'. And if your situation changes down the track, dip into the relevant section when the time is right for you.

Throughout the book, I've included lots of examples of questions you can ask your kids that will help you start conversations with them. Use them as you see fit.

Self-reflection is key to keeping yourself mentally prepared and on a positive path through your separation journey. Take time to read and reflect on the questions I have included in the book for you to consider. Please don't skip over these sections – sit somewhere quietly and really think about your answers to each of those questions.

Remember, you aren't chasing the 'parent of the year' award. You just need to regain your sanity, get your family back on track, and help your family to live their best lives. I hope you will keep this book on your bedside table as you step through your separation journey, as a guide to use when you need it most.

PART I

TELLING YOUR KIDS YOU ARE SEPARATING. YIKES.

'It's hard to tell your kids that you are getting a divorce. It's even harder to explain why, especially if you have a very different explanation and feeling about what happened from your co-parent.'

SO YOU'VE DECIDED TO SEPARATE. Or perhaps it wasn't your decision to end the relationship but you nevertheless find yourself in this situation. Here's the first truth bomb for you: someone is going to have to tell the kids.

Now if you're anything like me and you like to be on top of situations, or if you simply rock the 'tiger parent' mentality, your initial reaction will likely be to gather your little humans into your arms, tell them about the separation, and then get them thinking about the future.

Stop the bus, tiger parent ... and take a bit of time.

Take some time to reflect on how you are feeling but also how you think the separation is going to affect your children. Ask yourself whether your kids' perspective will differ from yours, and if so, how do you plan to handle that? Think about what the speed bump issues are going to be for your kids. What are the aspects of your separation that are going to make it difficult for your kids to come to terms with? This has a lot to do with each kid's maturity and stage of development.

And what about having the actual 'separation conversation' with them? What are you meant to say, and what should you be leaving *out* of the conversation?

In this part, I have given you some structure to help you know when to have this important conversation with your kids, how to frame the conversation and, most importantly, how to get help for your kids if they need it.

Chapter 1

KIDS HAVE DIFFERENT FEELINGS AND PERSPECTIVES

'Your job is to give your kids the space to live their feelings without being judged, corrected or interrupted.'

Before you have a conversation with your kids to tell them you are separating from their other parent, it helps to understand where your kids are at insofar as their emotional and physical needs. This chapter guides you about the different stages of development that kids go through, so you can work out what it is your kids need from you and how you should be breaking the news of your separation to them.

LET THEM HAVE THEIR FEELINGS AND DON'T TAKE IT PERSONALLY

If you find yourself in a situation where you are seriously contemplating a separation from your partner, or if you have already separated, you should know that your kids are going to be impacted. Please don't panic when you read this. It is altogether natural for your kids to feel anger, sadness and even fear when they hear about your plans.

How do you think your kids will react? Are you prepared for the conversation to fill them in on your separation? And if you have already shared the news, take a moment to reflect on what your kids' reactions were and ask yourself, do you know how they are truly feeling now?

Sometimes, kids may feel a sense of relief if there has been ongoing tension in the house, while others may get very quiet and leave you guessing what they are feeling.

There are lots of reasons why kids may have a hard time sharing their feelings with you. Often, they don't know how to express what they feel, while others may try to protect you from more upset or hurt.

Kids might also feel conflicted or confused if their feelings aren't in line with your own. Some kids may welcome a bit of peace in the home, while you are still reeling from the fallout of the separation.

Reassure your kids that it's okay if their feelings are not the same as yours. Let them know it's okay to feel whatever it is they are feeling. They might even have very different feelings from one moment to the next. This is natural and okay too.

It's normal for kids to feel angry or upset when they first learn about your separation. For them to move through these feelings and get to the other side, they need to know that you understand and accept how they are feeling. Do your best to practise empathy, and let your kids know that it's normal to feel angry and that you are willing to listen. Then help them come up with some healthy ways to handle their anger. Do your best not to take your kid's anger personally. Remember, it's not always all about you.

I don't mean to come across as bossy, but here's the thing: your job is to give your kids the space to live their feelings without being judged, corrected or interrupted. Do you think you can do that? If not, seek support because it's important for your kids to be secure in this space. Encourage your kids to talk and to ask for help when they have strong feelings. And when they do open up and talk to you, really listen to what they have to say. And make sure you remind them you love them, and you always will.

HELPING KIDS WITH THEIR FEELINGS

You can help your kids manage and move through difficult feelings by encouraging them to express their emotions in healthy and acceptable ways.

To help kids with sadness, suggest that they:

- talk to someone they trust
- draw or colour how they feel
- write in a journal
- take a walk
- sit in a safe and favourite place and think about things they love.

To handle anger, it helps if kids can:

- exercise
- step away from situations that cause strong feelings
- talk to a parent, friend or perhaps a school counsellor
- breathe deeply and count to 10 to calm themselves
- draw or write in a journal
- go outside or take a walk
- sit in a safe and favourite place and think about something that helps them calm down.

Leading by example can be a powerful way of helping kids cope with their feelings. You know that kids often learn more from what we do than what we say. If you want your kids to learn how to deal with difficult feelings or work on how to face challenges, lead by example. Let them see you paying attention to your own emotions, taking bad days in your stride, managing conflict with integrity, and turning to others for support when you need it.

While the big change brought about by separation may feel overwhelming for you and for your kids, you will all continue to learn new skills and strategies to get through the difficult period. Those skills and strategies will serve you and your kids well in life and make you all more confident, resilient and capable people. And that, my friends, is the silver lining of the splits.

THE EMOTIONAL STAGES OF LOSS FOR KIDS

The ride through divorce is like a rollercoaster, for both you and your children. What your kids feel today may be very different from what they will be feeling next week or next month. Let them know that it's normal to have ups and downs as they go through the process of healing. Do your best to reassure your kids that just as life changes, so do feelings, and in time things get much better.

The different feelings that kids may experience after they have learned about your divorce, and then moving onward through the process of separation and change, can be likened to grief.

In 1969, Elisabeth Kübler-Ross described five common stages of grief, often referred to as 'DABDA'. They are:

1. **D**enial
2. **A**nger
3. **B**argaining
4. **D**epression
5. **A**cceptance

Kübler-Ross's model was based on her work with terminally ill patients.

It is now widely accepted, however, that the stages of grief are not linear, and some people may not experience any of them. Others might only go through two stages or perhaps all five.

So, rather than thinking about the five stages of grief as a pathway that starts from one and ends at five, think about it as a group of stages that you, your co-parent and your kids may experience after separation. Much like this graphic.

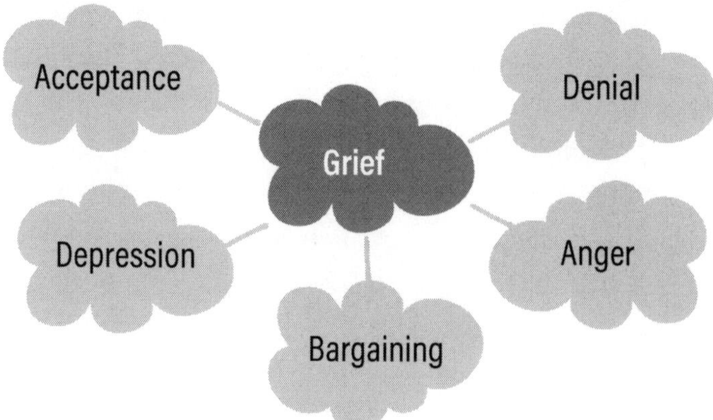

Having a general understanding of the grieving process will assist you in being alert to the feelings, reactions and behaviours of your kids once they join you on the separation journey. It will also help you to understand a bit better what you are going through and what it means to have the feelings you are experiencing.

Let's now get into the nuts and bolts of DABDA by looking briefly at each of the five stages, and what each stage might look like for your kids. And remember, they may not happen in this order, and not everybody will experience all of them.

1. Denial: this can't be happening to me

This is the stage that can initially help your kids to survive the loss of their family structure. At this stage, children might think life makes no sense, has no meaning and is too overwhelming.

Kids can start to deny the news and, in effect, go numb. They might not believe that you and their other parent have separated for good. It's common in this stage to wonder how life will look in the future. Kids might cling to the hope that you will get back together with your ex.

In the denial stage, kids tend to live in a 'preferable' reality. And often it is this denial that can help them to cope and survive for a time. Denial helps to pace their feelings. Instead of becoming completely overwhelmed with grief, kids can take some time by either denying the separation or refusing to accept it. It's kind of like the body's natural defence mechanism saying, 'hey, there's only so much I can handle at the moment'.

Once the denial starts to fade away, the start of the healing process begins. It's at this point that their feelings start to come to the surface, and it's about this time that you should strap in and get ready for the ride.

2. Anger: why is this happening and who can I blame?

Once children are living in actual reality and not in a 'preferable' reality, anger might start to set in. According to Kübler-Ross, this is a common stage to think, 'why me?', and, 'it's not fair'.

Kids might look to blame either you or your co-parent for the divorce, and they may even redirect their anger to friends and family. At this stage, kids can find it incomprehensible how something like this could happen to them.

Researchers and mental health professionals agree that this anger is a necessary stage of grief. It's actually important for your kids to go through this stage. It's not healthy to suppress feelings of anger. It's a natural response, and a necessary one.

It can be frustrating for kids because they are often told to control their anger. But these feelings can help to bind kids to reality and help to connect them to people again. It's a 'thing'. It's something for kids to hold on to and to talk about.

It's even more important to realise that the angry feelings will stop.

3. Bargaining: make this not happen, and in return I'll ...

When something bad happens in your life, have you ever caught yourself making a deal with yourself? I remember when my mum got sick with cancer back in 2015. I told myself that if she got better, I would try to be the best daughter ever and never be a problem for her. This is bargaining.

This stage is kind of like false hope. Kids might make themselves believe they can avoid the grief of separation with negotiation. If you and their other parent don't separate, they'll do everything they can to be the best kids you have ever met. Kids can be so desperate to get their life back, they can be willing to do almost anything.

During this stage they can start to think about endless 'what ifs'. What if I had eaten all my dinner each night? What if Mum didn't go on that holiday? What if Dad didn't work so hard? What if I didn't complain? What if, what if, what if? Imagine how exhausting these thoughts would be. Keep that in mind if you think your kids are going through this phase, and keep talking to them about their feelings.

4. Depression: I'm too sad to do anything

This is a stage that may seem a little scary, but I am not talking about clinical depression here. No parent wants to think that their kids are going to end up depressed after going through a divorce.

Try not to exaggerate this stage in your mind: keep calm and carry on reading.

Depression is a commonly accepted form of grief. It represents the emptiness we feel when we are living in reality and realise a relationship is over. In your kids' positions, it might be a realisation that their family has changed and things will not be the same as they were.

In this stage, kids can feel withdrawn and numb, and can feel like they are moving through a fog. It can all feel overwhelming, and in response, they can feel as though they don't want to be around others, they don't feel like talking or getting out of bed, and they might experience feelings of hopelessness.

If you think your children have moved into this stage and they are not coping, it's important to get some professional help from a counsellor or psychologist without delay.

5. Acceptance: I'm at peace with what happened

This stage is where kids start to realise and accept that they are going to be okay. In this stage, emotions can begin to stabilise.

Coming to terms with the new reality of their changed family structure gives kids the opportunity to move on and grow. It's definitely a time of adjustment and readjustment. There can be good days and sad days, and then there are good days again.

This doesn't mean your kids will never have another sad day. But, the good days tend to outnumber the sad days. Kids can start to feel as though they are floating out of the fog and you might see them engaging energetically with friends again, and even making new relationships.

* * *

Pulling the stages together

There are five stages of grief and your kids may go through all of the stages or perhaps only a few. There is no linear way that kids will work through these. The best you can do is to try to understand the stage your kids are going through and how best you can support them through it.

Remind your kids you will always love them. And so will your ex.

You may be reading this and thinking, *Of course Bron, I will be telling my kids I love them every day*. But what I mean here is, tell them that you will *always* love them. It's different to telling them daily that you love them.

Let me explain.

Divorce shows kids that love doesn't always last. Your kids may wonder, *If my parents can stop loving each other, will they stop loving me too?*

I think I just saw your lightbulb moment happen.

Kids need to know that the love you have for them is a 'forever love' – different from the kind of love you once shared with their other parent.

CONVERSATIONS TO HAVE ABOUT FEELINGS

Focus on giving your children the space they need to have their own feelings about changes in the family, including the really hard ones.

Take some time to reflect on these questions:

- If you have already talked to your kids about separating from their other parent, how did they react to the news?
- If you haven't told them yet, what can you do to prepare for their reactions?
- What are some ways that you can help manage your kids' anger?
- What might be some healthy ways for your kids to manage their sadness?
- How comfortable are you with your kids' anger or sadness?
- What are some things you can do to keep your own feelings separate from your kids' feelings, so that you can truly support them?
- What kind of supports do you need to organise so you can really be there for your kids?

Divorce brings up a lot of feelings. Talk to your kids and share with them these five truths about feelings:

- **Truth #1: You can't stop feelings** no matter how hard you try. So don't fight your feelings. Let your feelings come and let them go.
- **Truth #2: Ignoring your feelings doesn't make them go away.** When you allow yourself to feel your feelings and let them out, you will feel so much better. But it's important that you make good choices about how you handle your feelings. For example, it might be okay to be angry at your brother, but it's not okay to hit him. A better choice could be to walk away and cool off, talk to a parent, or take the dog for a walk.
- **Truth #3: Feelings change.** You may not feel it now, but every feeling passes sooner or later, some sooner than others. But they all move on eventually. Except love. Love can stay forever.

- **Truth #4: You have the right to feel any way you want.** You don't have to have the same feelings as your parents. It's okay to feel happy, even if your parents are feeling sad or angry. And it's okay to still feel sad when your parents begin to feel happier. It's your right.
- **Truth #5: Find a buddy.** Everyone needs someone to talk to from time to time. If you can't talk to one of your parents, find someone you trust to help you sort through the tough stuff.

After you have shared the five truths with your kids, you might like to have a discussion with your kids about the following:

- What can you do to make yourself feel better when you are feeling angry or frustrated?
- Do you ever feel *really* angry? What do you do when you feel that way?
- Do you ever feel *really* sad? What do you do when you feel that way?
- What can help you to feel better again?
- Do you think divorce is unfair?
- Do you ever worry about one of us leaving forever?
- Are there other things that you worry about?

Before you launch into any conversations with your kids about your separation, take the time to consider their emotional and physical needs. Think about what stages of development each of your kids are at, so that you can be well informed about how you should break the news of your separation to them.

Chapter 2

UNDERSTANDING WHERE YOUR KIDS ARE AT BEFORE THE 'DIVORCE TALK'

'No pressure, but if you're a parent, you are a key influencer in your kids' lives. With that comes great responsibility.'

THE POTENTIAL SPEED BUMPS FOR KIDS

In this chapter, I will give you an overview of the challenges that can arise (aka the speed bumps) when you are negotiating the balancing act of continuing a healthy relationship with your kids at the same time as a separation from your partner.

The Australian parenting website, Raisingchildren.net.au, is an invaluable resource for learning more about your kids' social, emotional and physical development, and many of the ideas below are supported by this helpful resource. Supported by the Australian Government Department of Social Services, Parenting Research Centre, The Royal Children's Hospital Melbourne and the Murdoch Children's Research Institute, the site is full of advice and ideas about raising healthy kids. If you get the time and have not done so already, do yourself a favour and bookmark the site.

It would be remiss of me, however, to leave it at that. I don't hold any formal qualifications in child and adolescent development. However, along with my research from reputable sources as well as my time as a family lawyer and Independent Children's Lawyer, a primary school teacher, and a mother to three teenagers, I have included some important things you may wish to think about regarding your children if your family has separated.

The content in this chapter is not intended as a substitute for professional consultation with a qualified practitioner, and if any information included here causes you concern, you should seek advice from your family medical practitioner or a psychologist.

BUT FIRST, A WORD OF ADVICE

If you're reading this book and you have older kids, you don't need me to tell you that kids go through distinct periods of development. And if you're a new parent, hold on for the ever-changing, never-boring parenting journey.

It's not my intention to spout advice about child development. But, my thought is that it can be helpful to remind you of the ages and stages of child development as a way of reflecting back on what you have already been through, and perhaps to think about what's coming next in your parenting journey.

When it comes to separation and divorce, and talking about it with your kids, planning is key. Without a plan you run the risk of jumping into the abyss of mayhem, tears, fears and crazy times. And none of us want that. No, we want as smooth and calm a transition into your new family life as possible. And I think reading this chapter will help to remind you of the amazing growth but also the difficult everyday transitions that your children, pre-teens or teenagers are facing. Keep this in mind when you are planning how you are going to move through your separation journey. And keep this in mind when you are planning on breaking the news to your kids.

THE AGES AND STAGES OF DEVELOPMENT FOR KIDS

Kids go through distinct periods of development as they grow from infants to young adults. During each stage, many changes in the development of their brains are taking place. The changes that occur and when they occur are genetically determined. However, environmental factors and experiences with key humans within their environment have a significant influence on how your kids benefit from each developmental event.

It's important that you keep in mind what stage of development your children are at when you are going through separation, as this will impact how they respond to the separation and should also inform you about how to talk to your kids about the separation. I've included a brief summary below of the key developmental issues your kids will experience and how those may impact responses to separation.

What developmental issues are important to consider when your family is separating?

Infants (birth to two years) and toddlers (18 months to three years)

> Sally and Roger had an amicable separation. Their baby boy, Declan, lived with his mum (who was still breastfeeding) and spent lots of short periods of time with his dad. Sally and Roger agreed that Declan was too young to spend extended periods or overnight time away from Sally. They also agreed that they would revisit this routine when Declan turned three.

If you are going through the splits when your kids are babies or toddlers, they can experience significant risk if they spend extended periods of time away from their primary carer. It's important to ensure your kids do not experience distress due to separation from whomever is the primary carer. The primary carer is the parent who spends the majority of time with the infant or toddler. Often the mother is the primary carer – this is especially so if she has taken time off work to care for the infant or toddler and has been primarily responsible for feeding and generally caring for them. However, it is not unusual for a father to be a primary carer.

Even though it's important for your kids to not experience distress at separation from the primary carer, it's also important that your kids are given the opportunity to develop meaningful relationships with both parents. However, if your children experience distress from being away from you or your co-parent, there can be ongoing and lifelong risks for them. It is because of this that the primary carer should be given priority at this stage of development.

Preschoolers (three to six years)

> When Michael and his wife, Joanne, separated, their two children, Bryce, six, and Kylie, four, were already used to being with their dad most of the time, since their mum's job kept her travelling all but a few days a month. When Joanne moved out of their home, it took a while for Kylie to understand the change. When the kids got home from their first weekend with their mum, Kylie said, 'Mummy home?' even though they had just left her. It will take Kylie time and lots of simple explanations before she can understand her new routine.

At this stage of development, kids are just starting to become more equipped to cope with separating from their primary carer and to spend more substantial time across two homes. This is because they are beginning to express themselves properly and can be reassured through conversations. It's also because kids of this age can understand the notion of time and can start to predict and expect events to happen regularly.

You should keep in mind though that pre-schoolers tend to be egocentric and see themselves as the centre of their universe. They can find it hard to work out the difference between their real and imaginary worlds, and can become confused about what is happening. Pre-schoolers can sometimes feel they are responsible for the separation.

School-agers and tweens (6 to 12 years)

> Lisa recalls her daughter Ruby, then in Year One, trying to understand the conflicts behind her parents' separation. Lisa recalls a time when Ruby asked her, 'Why are you fighting? Is it because Dad deleted something from your laptop?' This misunderstanding was easily fixed. Yes, Ruby's father had deleted something from Lisa's laptop and they had angry words about it, but, of course, that did not cause the divorce. However, her daughter's question made Lisa realise Ruby's need to make sense of circumstances she couldn't fully understand.

As kids reach school age, they have a much better capacity to regulate their emotions and manage themselves independently. They can spend more time away from their primary carer as they continue to develop their social and interpersonal skills. They want to be kept in the loop, so be ready to give your tween age-appropriate updates about future plans.

Teenagers (13 to 18 years)

> June's boys were 13 and 15 when she went through a messy divorce from her alcoholic husband. The situation was so bad that, at one point, both parents were ordered by the judge not to discuss court proceedings with their boys. It's impossible to completely shield kids from that type of conflict, but June did what she could: 'I just tried to make our home a safe haven. We had regular bedtimes and meals and my husband was never allowed in the home. When I left the boys to go out in the evening, I took my mobile phone and told them to call me any time.'
>
> And they did call her, often. Her eldest son, Peter, started getting headaches and having trouble sleeping. June said, 'I was worried that, given my stress, I couldn't do enough on my own to give him the coping skills to get help.' Peter started seeing a counsellor, who made a big difference and really helped him.

Even though it seems as though your teenager is moving ahead in leaps and bounds with their social and emotional development, they still have many vulnerabilities that can be exacerbated during separation.

Your teen might see the world in absolutes. For example, that something is either 'all wonderful' or 'all really bad'. Your teenager is also vulnerable to emotional influence and suggestions. Because of this, they might feel that they have to side with you if they think you are particularly vulnerable, or they may want to 'fix everything'.

Watch for any emotional or social regression from your teen, as this can occur if they become overly dependent on you (or your co-parent) at the expense of their own individual capacity to get through the separation.

The changes that kids are experiencing in their thinking

Young kids are curious, easily distracted and constantly striving for independence. Giving them the independence they so desperately desire can be difficult though, because young kids are still developing self-regulation. As young kids get better at self-regulation, they learn to get along with others and to think about how to be cooperative.

The pre-teen and teen years see lots of big changes, including physical, emotional, cognitive and social changes. During this time, kids' bodies, emotions and identities change in different ways at different times.

Pre-teens and teens may start to go through a stage of acting without thinking. Remember, their decision-making skills are still developing and they are still learning that actions have consequences – and even risks sometimes.

Your pre-teen's body is maturing physically but their brain development and thinking skills are developing at a different speed. What you see on the surface (their physical appearance) doesn't always match what's happening inside.

The changes that kids are experiencing in their emotions

Kids learn and develop best when they have strong, loving and positive relationships with their parents. That's because those positive relationships help them to learn about their world. They learn to work out whether their world is safe and secure, whether they're loved, who loves them, what happens when they laugh, get angry or cry.

Once your kids get to around 9 to 10 years of age, you might notice that they can show strong feelings and intense emotions at different times. Moods might seem unpredictable, and these emotional ups and downs can lead to increased conflict with any siblings, and with you and their other parent.

At the same time, your kids can be more sensitive to your emotions. As they get older, teenagers start to get a better understanding of other people's emotions, but they can sometimes misread facial expressions or body language. This can lead to reacting in unexpected ways.

The changes that kids are experiencing socially

When your kids are very young their focus is mainly on you, their brothers and sisters, and other humans who come in and out of their direct world. By around three years of age, as they start to regularly do activities with other kids their age, they start to develop the concept of friendship. Some kids can make friends easily and they get energy from being around lots of other people. Other kids can find this tiring and overwhelming. Some kids can be slower to warm up, and giving them time to watch what happens before joining a group can help them to be emotionally ready.

As they get older, pre-teens are busy working out who they are and where they fit into the world. You might have noticed that your pre-teen is searching for their own identity. As an example, you might find that they are trying out new or different fashion looks, art, music and friendship groups.

At this stage, seeking more independence is common and healthy. You might notice that your pre-teen wants to get to school on their own or spend more time with friends. They might want to be, and are ready for, more responsibility both at home and at school.

Your pre-teen or teen is probably looking for new experiences. And those experiences can be risky ones too. At the same time, your pre-teen is developing control over their impulses, and this has a lot to do with the way their brain is changing at this time.

Right now, you may be thinking, *this sounds great. Could be the perfect age for the separation journey?* You might be right. Your pre-teen or teen is likely to be thinking more about 'right' and 'wrong', and will even be starting to develop their own values and morals. They will be questioning things more.

It's a good idea to remember that your words and actions shape your kids' sense of right and wrong, as do your co-parent's words and actions. So too does the online world. The internet, mobile phones and social media can all significantly influence how your pre-teen or teen communicates with their friends and how they learn about the world.

It's also common to find your older kids being influenced more by friends, especially around their behaviour, sense of self and their self-esteem.

The relationship changes that kids are experiencing

Work on building positive relationships with your kids by being in the moment, spending quality time with them and creating a caring environment of trust and respect. There is no formula for getting your relationship with them right. But if your relationship is built on warm, loving and responsive interactions, your kids will feel loved and secure.

Young kids are starting to make friends and develop relationships outside the family unit. But they need role models and support to develop friendship skills such as sharing, taking turns, being cooperative, listening and sorting out disagreements.

As young kids play with others, they build the skills that will help them with friendships now and in the future. They are learning what's okay in friendships. Some young kids might tell others they can't join in their group, or say things like, 'You're not my friend'. You might also catch your young children making bargains or threats around friendships, such as, 'If you don't invite me to your birthday party, I won't be your friend'.

Some young kids can be hurt by this behaviour, and other kids can simply shake it off and move on to the Play-Doh. If your young kids talk about ongoing problems playing with friends at preschool it can be a good idea to talk to their teacher. The teachers can keep an eye out and help with modelling good friendship traits.

Your pre-teen's and teen's relationships with you, their wider family and their friends will go through lots of shifts. It's important for your pre-teen or teen to keep strong relationships with both family and friends, to ensure healthy social and emotional development. This can be difficult when your family is going through a separation.

Even for pre-teens and teens who aren't going through separation, wanting to spend less time with family and more time with friends can be common. Your pre-teen's or teen's friends can have a strong influence over their interests and daily choices, like:

- what sports they are interested in
- what music they listen to
- what they are wearing when they go out
- what movies they are watching.

Don't worry about this. It's all part and parcel of them finding their feet in the world. And don't forget, it's your influence that is important for your kids' long-term decisions, like deciding on a career, their values and their morals. Their short-term decisions, although important, are not the be all and end all.

You may find you argue more with your pre-teen or teen than when they were younger. This is normal as they look to find their independence. It actually shows that your kids are maturing. Even if you feel like you're arguing with your pre-teen or teen all the time, try not to be concerned. It isn't likely to affect your relationship with them in the longer term.

It also might seem like your pre-teen or teen sees things differently from you now. This can be especially so after a separation, and when they argue with you about what is best for them. Your kids don't see things differently to upset you or to be combative. It's because they're beginning to think more abstractly at this stage of development and are questioning different points of view.

ROLE CONFUSION FOR KIDS DURING SEPARATION

Kids can easily be drawn into taking on an adult role in an effort to keep the peace. This is especially so with teens or younger kids who are known for their organisational and peacekeeping skills.

Help your kids to understand that the problems you have with your co-parent are your problems and not theirs.

To avoid kids getting pulled into adult roles like the carer or peacemaker, reassure them that when you and your co-parent get angry at each other, it's not their job to make things better. Explain that it is your job to find a way to work things out. Make sure your kids understand that their feelings don't have to be the same as your or your co-parent's feelings. And discuss with your children that they can't fix or change how their parents feel or behave. The only person they can take responsibility for is themselves.

YOU'VE GOT THIS

Remember, you've got this. Arming yourself with information about what stage of development your kids are at when you separate will help you immensely in figuring out the next best steps for how you talk to your kids about the separation and what to say to them about the future. You can navigate a calm and sensible pathway for them through your family separation. Find yourself a positive mantra and repeat it three times every morning. You could try something like this:

> I am strong. I will remain calm. I've got this.
> I am strong. I will remain calm. I've got this.
> I am strong. I will remain calm. I've got this.

* * *

After reading this chapter I expect you will have a clearer understanding of the speed bumps that can arise when you are working through how to continue a healthy relationship with your kids and how best to prepare them for separation. Separation and divorce can be a very stressful time for families. By understanding how your kids might react to different scenarios and conversations about separation, you will empower yourself to prepare for a smoother ride along the road to your new lives.

Chapter 3

THE CONVERSATION

'Have faith in your ability to know what's best for your kids and move forward with the confidence that you will keep their best interests at heart - always.'

You and your ex have decided to split. Or perhaps it's not a decision you have made together but it's happening anyway. If you're lucky, the situation is amicable and you may have already discussed the big stuff like where you are all going to live and how, the arrangements for splitting your assets, and who's keeping Rufus, the family dog.

So, I guess it's time to tell the kids. This is where you might hear the proverbial 'crickets chirping', or start to have visions of tumbleweeds blowing through the desert.

But do not fear, my friend. I've included a guide for you to help you figure out the best way to break the news. And let's face it, depending on their age, some kids will already instinctively know something's not right.

Let's get to it.

INTRODUCING THE IDEA OF SEPARATION TO YOUR KIDS

When parents split up, kids worry about what their new lives will be like. Will they still see their relatives from both sides of the family?

Will they go to the same school and have the same friends? Will they still get to visit family friends every Christmas holiday?

A common theme that runs through these concerns is a fear of *change*. How do you talk to your kids about change?

It helps to get your kids 'ready' for change. They've experienced change in the past, and it's this concept that they need to accept about your separation. When you prepare your kids for a big change – such as their other parent moving out of the family home – think about how you have previously helped your kids handle changes.

Also consider how you would manage other changes in their lives. If your kids were transferring to a new school, how would you get them ready for that? What would you do to help them prepare for the first day? Instead of just dropping them off at the school gate, you might tour the school with them or have a conversation about what the first day might look like.

Think about how you could take a similar approach to the family changes your kids are going through now. Be sure to balance explaining the changes with reassurances about important things that will stay the same. Depending on the age of your kids, you might like to try something like:

> You know how trees grow and clouds move through the sky? And even rocks change over the years? Well, some changes happen slowly, and they are hard to see. But other changes come with a bang.
>
> Change can feel really good, but it can also feel really uncomfortable ... especially at first. Even grown ups can feel uncomfortable or worried when things change, especially if the change is a surprise.

Focus on explaining that parents separate for a lot of different reasons, and when they separate, it's natural for kids to want to understand what is happening to their family. Let your kids know that it's okay to ask questions. But also let them know that they may not get all their questions answered, and they may not get the answers they want.

Explain to your kids that this is because even though it's their family and they may feel they deserve to know everything (especially teenagers), some things are really just for parents. And sometimes parents themselves don't even understand what happened to their marriage, so it can be hard to answer some questions.

WHEN IS THE BEST TIME FOR THE CONVERSATION?

It's very hard to tell your kids that you are getting a divorce. It's even harder to explain why, especially if you have a very different explanation and feeling about what happened compared to your co-parent.

Your kids, however, are really paying attention to everything going on around them, and they are probably trying very hard to make sense of what's happening. They hear the arguments and feel the tension at home. So, when you don't give them answers, they will likely create their own stories.

I'm hearing you say to me, 'But *when* is the right time to drop the bomb? *When* should I tell my kids?'

It can be seriously difficult to get the timing right. Say, for example, you've decided with your co-parent to take a break from the relationship but you haven't yet reached a definitive decision about separating. Should you tell your kids? What if your other half has just upped and left and you have been completely blindsided? You may not have the capacity to handle the situation yourself, let alone share the news with your kids.

The answer to these questions is to just be truthful and to keep your children updated about the facts. For example, if your co-parent has left and you're not sure what's going to happen next, tell your kids that their mum or dad is having some time out, and reassure them that you will keep explaining to them what is happening as best you can. Also tell them you both love them and always will.

You should also consider the age and maturity of your kids (see chapter 2). Have faith in your ability to know what's best for them and move forward with the confidence that you will keep their best interests at heart - always.

KEEP IT SIMPLE ... AND REAL

Your kids will want to understand what is happening, but be careful not to give them more information than they can handle. Don't share details about personal issues, problems in your marriage, your feelings about your co-parent, legal matters or child support. This kind of information can lead your kids to becoming upset, anxious, confused and fearful for their future. Most of all, your kids want to hear that everybody will be okay and that you will always love them.

From my experience as a family lawyer and Independent Children's Lawyer, and also as a primary school teacher who has had my fair share of conversations with kids about separation, kids do best when you can give them a reasonable, truthful, non-blaming explanation for your separation.

For younger kids (eight years and younger), you can say something like:

> We both love you very much. It's just that we aren't happy living together anymore, so we've decided to live in separate homes. We will always love you and we will always be a family.

For older kids, they might need to hear something like:

> Sometimes in a marriage, feelings change. Usually it's not just one big thing but lots of smaller things that build up over time. We know it's probably hard for you to understand this. Perhaps you are even wondering if we can fix this. We want you to know that our decision to split up was really hard. We know this is difficult for you. We're so sorry this is hard for you.

You should also try to make sure you talk to your kids about:

- what will change and what will stay the same
- what divorce means
- where they will live and go to school, if this is changing
- when and how they will see each parent, if you have worked this out – even just for the short term.

If your kids are very young when you separate, remember that they may need to rethink the divorce as they get older. What made sense to them when they were seven years old may no longer work for them when they are 13. So be prepared for questions about your separation to be raised along the way, and into the future.

And keep in mind that, though they may be older, it doesn't necessarily mean you should bare your soul and tell your kids everything. Even older kids still need a buffer from the details of your relationship. Although logically they understand so much more, emotionally they may not be prepared to handle some information.

ONE PARENT OR TWO?

Kids benefit from hearing the same message from both parents whenever possible.

In a perfect world, your co-parent will sit down with you and discuss how you are going to tell the kids about the separation. Some of those discussion points could be:

- when the kids should be told
- what they should be told about why the separation happened
- whether you will tell the kids together or separately.

Telling your kids together, if done calmly and lovingly, can help send a strong message to your kids that although you are no longer living together as a family, they will always be loved and they will always have a family.

Of course, if you are unable to have a civil conversation with your ex, it is not appropriate to force a family meeting to break the news, where animosity and negative feelings may surface. Don't risk it. Take on the responsibility to update your kids yourself as soon as appropriate and explain to your co-parent that you are doing this.

DON'T PLAY THE BLAME GAME

We've all done it before. We've had an argument, felt pretty upset about it, and downloaded on another human to air our grievances. But in a family separation – one of the most stressful events in your life – I implore you to stay away from blame, as hard as that may seem at times.

Telling your kids that the divorce is the other parent's fault (even if that is your truth) will leave your kids feeling confused and caught in the middle. It will increase their anxiety and their discomfort. Playing the blame game may make your kids feel like they need to take sides, and that is a slippery slope indeed.

BE PREPARED FOR THE HARD QUESTIONS

Kids are naturally inquisitive. They want to know why things are so, what is happening, when it's going to happen and who is involved.

Kids are wonderers. They are curious, and they often know a lot more than we think they do. When something big happens, they want to understand why it happened. Without an explanation, their imaginations can run wild as they try to make sense of it all. And sadly, the answers they dream up might be more upsetting to them than the real thing.

Don't leave them hanging, and be ready for the hard questions. In fact, it's a good idea to invite their questions. Whenever you talk to your kids about your separation or any related changes that have occurred or will occur, remember to ask them if they have any questions. Tell your kids you want to hear all their questions, even the hard ones.

If your kids have questions you're not ready or able to answer, it's okay to tell them you don't have everything figured out yet. But reassure them that when you have an answer, they'll be the first to know. If your kids keep asking for details you feel they shouldn't have, you can say something like:

> I know it's hard to understand why this happened, and you probably still have some questions. I'll do my best to answer you. And you need to know that there are some things about the divorce that are just between Mum and Dad.

When it comes to explaining 'why', there is probably no magic answer and you may never be able to completely satisfy your kids' desire to know. Your kids might keep asking 'why?', or may want more details that you are not comfortable sharing with them. Try to keep your explanations of the separation simple, honest and consistent. And remember they don't need to hear all the details.

Think about the following questions your kids could ask you and what your responses might be:

- Where's Mum gone?
- Who's going to make dinner?
- Why don't you love Dad any more?
- Will you get back together?
- What do I tell my friends?
- Why are you crying?
- Is Dad coming to my birthday party?

Importantly, it's a really good idea to tell your kids that it's *not* their fault ... and then tell them again. Some kids can feel responsible for the separation. Tell your kids they did nothing wrong. Explain that a divorce is between parents. It's not their job to fix things. Reassure your kids again and again that they are not to blame, as many times as you need to.

WHAT'S YOUR ELEVATOR PITCH?

After reflecting on this chapter, and perhaps even re-reading it, I'm hoping you've reached the conclusion that you need to prepare and absolutely get your story straight before you talk to your kids about the separation.

Here is an exercise I use with my clients when they ask me for help about how to break the news of their separation to the kids:

1. Write the story of your divorce in just four lines.
2. Now write the story again, without placing any blame on either you or your ex.
3. Next, write a list of what you think your kids need to know right now about the divorce.
4. Also write a second list of what would be hurtful for your kids to know, even if for you it is true.
5. Now, write your story again in four lines, taking into consideration the earlier steps, in a way that feels true for you but also keeps your kids' best interests in mind.

Congratulations. You've just written your divorce elevator pitch. Learn it off by heart and use it when required.

WHAT SHOULD YOUR KIDS TELL THEIR FRIENDS?

Here's a reality check. In 2019, the Australian Bureau of Statistics found that 113,815 marriages were registered and 49,116 divorces were granted in Australia. It works out to be that almost one in every two marriages fails. And that figure doesn't include de facto relationships.

Even though divorce is more common than ever, and the chances are fairly high that your kids will know someone whose parents have separated, kids still struggle with feeling different. They can worry about what others think about their changing family.

Spending time talking to them about what they might want to share with their friends can be really helpful. You could suggest a short, simple explanation that feels okay for your family, like:

> My parents are separating and they're still working things out.

Or:

> I have two homes. Part of the week I live with my Mum and the other part with my Dad.

Talk to your kids about it being okay if they don't want to talk about separation with their friends or other people outside of the family. Let them know it's okay to just say, 'Thanks for asking, but I don't want to talk about it right now.'

TIPS TO HELP YOU PREPARE FOR THE CONVERSATION

It's often the great unknown that's the most frightening thing for kids. You can help smooth the way by keeping your kids informed whenever possible about changes that are going to happen. Don't avoid talking about your divorce, even if you feel uncomfortable.

Here are some ways to prepare for the conversation with your kids about the change in their family life:

1. Plan what you want to say before talking with your kids.
2. Give your kids age-appropriate information.
3. Focus on their feelings.
4. Be as clear as possible about what will change and what will stay the same.
5. Whenever possible, give your kids time to adjust to the idea of what will change before the change actually happens.
6. If your kids have questions you're not ready or able to answer, it's okay to tell them that you don't have everything figured out yet. But reassure them that when you have an answer, they'll be the first to know.
7. Remember, keeping kids informed doesn't mean sharing every detail with them. Your kids still need to be protected from adult information like the reasons why you separated, child support, legal stuff and money concerns.

Reflect on the following questions to help yourself prepare for a conversation with your kids about divorce:

- How much do you think your kids need to know about why you have separated?

- What are some things that you think your kids are better off not hearing about?
- What might your kids still be wondering about?
- Have you asked your kids if they have any questions about the separation?
- Are there more things you can talk to them about now that would help them make sense of the separation?
- Have you spoken to your co-parent about having a consistent explanation for the separation, for the kids' sake?

Chapter 4

WHEN AND HOW TO GET HELP FOR YOUR KIDS

'Many parents that I have met in my years practising as a family lawyer have told me they feel guilty about their divorce and what they have put their kids through.'

It doesn't take a genius to figure out that divorce will impact your children. Difficulties are to be expected and are common. But how do you know when the impact is bordering on being too much for your kids? And what can you do about helping them?

BE READY TO ACT

You know your kids better than anyone. Going through a family separation, you'll likely be diligent in your surveillance of your kids' emotions. Be aware that their age and personality will affect how they respond to the news of your separation. But in general, these are some common feelings your kids may have:

- sadness
- confusion
- fear
- relief

- anger
- worry
- acceptance.

It's important to recognise that these feelings are all part of the rollercoaster of emotions your kids may experience because of your separation.

As well as being sensitive towards their feelings and giving them plenty of love and support, you should be aware of what to do when you start to have a niggle about your kids' behaviour that may then move towards a full blown concern.

The key to considering your concerns about your kids' feelings, and staying on top of any major issues, is awareness. Find ways to document your concerns, and if you see a pattern emerging or a behaviour that starts as a minor concern and then becomes a major one, be ready to act.

> Around three years ago, a young mum came to see me, seeking assistance because her husband had unexpectedly left the family home to start a new life with another family. It was a very sad situation – the mum had no inclination as to what had happened, or why.
>
> Her confusion and sadness were evident to me as I gently offered a box of tissues to her and asked her to talk to me about her twin boys. The boys were, at that time, 11 years of age. According to my client, they were very angry at their Dad for leaving. One of the boys, Timothy, was particularly angry and upset, and he had become aggressive towards his twin brother. My client said to me, 'they usually fight like little tigers but lately, Timothy has become like an enraged bull'. When I suggested to her that the boys might both benefit from some counselling, she quickly said to me, 'Oh no. It's not that bad'.

Now, what does that mean – 'it's not that bad'? Was Timothy's behaviour 'not that bad' for my client to deal with, or was it that

Timothy's anger wasn't a concern for her? The fact is, the way Timothy was acting towards his twin brother had changed, and likely for good reason. He was trying to process an intense situation, and as an 11-year-old he simply did not have the skills or maturity to handle it.

As my conversation with the young mum continued, I learned that she had never been to counselling and she thought that it meant she would be pressured to put her son on medication, or worse, be admitted to hospital.

This story is a good example of the importance of taking concerns seriously, even if they are only niggles, and arming yourself with the right information to understand when and where to seek help. Be aware of the support services available to you, and don't be afraid to take action or steps to find out more.

If you notice your children being worryingly affected by the changes in your home after separation, let them know they can contact the Kids Helpline on 1800 55 1800 and talk to a counsellor. This is a free service.

There are some excellent resources out there for you to tap into if you think your kids need help. Let's say you have a niggle - a feeling that won't go away - that there is something going on with your kids. The feeling grows and grows but you just can't quite put your finger on whether your niggle is just you being overly sensitive to the situation, or whether your niggle is a precursor to a fully blown issue.

Kids Helpline have a useful app that can help you to manage your niggles, called 'Niggle'. This app is actually designed for kids to use, but from my experience it's also a helpful tool for parents who are navigating separation with their kids.

It's an app that you can also absolutely share with your children because it's designed for them. It gives them the tools to make decisions about whether their niggles are more than just that. But it is also a resource you can use to keep track of concerning behaviours. I highly recommend you and your kids download this free app onto your phones. The link to the Niggle app can be found on the Kids

Helpline website, which is www.kidshelpline.com.au. The website explains how Niggle can help you and your kids:

> Track your wellbeing and get personalised information, videos, podcasts, quizzes and tips to help you tame your niggles. Plus, hear from other young people as they share their stories and find out what helped them! From feeling down or sad to sexual identity, dealing with conflict, loneliness and more – this is your take home, self-help toolkit that is here for you 24/7 for all things related to mental, social and emotional wellbeing.

While you can't control the way your kids feel about your separation, you can take precautions to monitor their behaviour, and get them help when they need it. And remember to look after yourself too. It's okay for you to feel overwhelmed or unsure about what to do next if you have concerns about your kids.

KNOWING WHEN TO ACT IMMEDIATELY

There can be some concerning signs your kids might display that you should be aware of, like aggression or depression. But usually, it is persistent, ongoing negative behaviour that you will be alerted to. This can creep up on you if the behaviour is slowly escalating.

Stay in touch with your kids' teachers, coaches and other adults who spend time with them so you can stay up to date about their behaviour outside of home.

Keeping a diary of your concerns about your kids' behaviours and using apps like Niggle can help you to record and remember what has been happening lately. This can become important information to share with a professional if you notice that a certain worrying behaviour persists.

If possible, keep communicating with your co-parent about behaviour issues. It might be that only one of you notices a certain behaviour taking place in your home, while your co-parent may notice something completely different. Recognising these different reactions to various environmental stressors can greatly assist you in giving your kids the right help and support.

But when to act is the question. When should you take behaviour issues or emotional changes seriously and do something about it?

If you notice issues starting to crop up with your kids, it's best to do something about it as quickly as possible. Many parents I have met in my years practising as a family lawyer have told me they feel guilty about their divorce and what they have put their kids through. That guilt often leads parents to let certain negative behaviours in their kids slide after separation - behaviours like answering back, not following your rules or even just refusing to have dinner with the family. By allowing these smaller negative behaviours to continue they can be reinforced and worsened, and this can have a long-term impact on your kids' wellbeing and emotional health.

Some behaviour issues will only be evident in your kids for short periods of time, and as long as you are aware of and tracking that behaviour, often those behaviours can naturally (and often quickly) dissipate.

But in some cases, where the behaviour is suddenly bad enough for you to sit up and say to yourself, 'Whoa, what happened there?', or has persisted long enough to concern you, seeking professional help is the best thing to offer your kids.

Counsellors, therapists and other mental health professionals are trained and have the knowledge to help your kid if they are suffering from behavioural issues. Sometimes, your kids might even feel more comfortable opening up about their feelings to a professional who is not directly involved in their home life.

A professional may also be able to diagnose if something more serious is happening and possibly affecting the health of your children. Only a trained professional can diagnose issues such as mental illness (which can include anxiety, depression and suicidal ideation) - don't try to diagnose or treat persistent issues on your own.

And don't forget about stress. Stress is a significant issue for children who are experiencing a family separation, and it has a profound effect on their mental state. If you can see that your kids are stressed out, get some help for them.

Behaviours to watch out for

If you notice sudden onset of or ongoing, persistent behaviours that indicate your kids are suffering from stress or emotional turmoil they cannot manage on their own, you should seek immediate help for them. Some common symptoms to be aware of are:

- Regressive behaviour, or when behaviour is not appropriate for their age. Examples of regressive behaviours in older children are thumb sucking, throwing tantrums, engaging in baby-talk, and not being able to sleep without a nightlight.
- New or recurring fears that might manifest as nightmares or even phobias.
- An inability to relax or calm down.
- Trouble controlling their emotions.
- Drastic changes in mood, behaviour or personality.
- Significant changes in eating habits.
- Significant weight loss or weight gain.
- Frequent headaches or stomachaches.
- Changes in school performance, or avoiding or missing school.
- Persistent sadness for two or more weeks.
- Withdrawing from their friends, or avoiding social interactions.
- Hurting themselves or talking about hurting themselves.
- Talking about death or suicide.

I've included a helpful infographic opposite that summarises nine signs of possible mental health issues. Use this infographic as a quick guide to help you think about whether you need to seek further help for your kids. The infographic was created by Health Direct, an Australian Government initiative, to assist in understanding mental health issues.

Nine signs of mental illness

Derived from: http://media.healthdirect.org.au/publications/new-9-signs-of-mental-illness-infographic.pdf

WHERE TO FIND HELP

If you think your kids are struggling with your separation and they need extra support, a good place to start is to speak with your local GP. Your GP can help you to find appropriate support, such as with local counsellors and psychologists.

You should be ready to talk to your GP about the behaviours that are concerning you. Also speak to your kids' teachers, close friends, relatives and any other caregivers to see if they've noticed changes in behaviour, and be ready to share this information with your GP.

Your GP can provide your kid with a mental health care plan, in which they will identify what type of health care your kid needs and set out what you and your GP have agreed you are aiming to achieve for your kid.

SHOULD MY KIDS SEE A COUNSELLOR OR A PSYCHOLOGIST?

Counsellors listen to people talk about their feelings, without judging or offering advice. They can help you or your kids to better understand yourself/themselves, solve problems, reach goals and develop self-worth.

Counsellors can have different backgrounds, specialisations and qualifications. Some have formal qualifications in counselling, some can be registered psychologists, and others have backgrounds in teaching, nursing, psychology or social work.

They can offer a mix of one-on-one counselling, family therapy and group work for children and families, all depending on your situation.

Alternatively, you might consider a psychologist. Psychologists are university-trained health professionals who study human behaviour. They are experts in the ways people think, feel, learn and behave.

Most psychologists work with people when they are upset or troubled, for example when someone is experiencing signs of anxiety or depression. They also work alongside people who are going through challenges in life, like relationship or parenting issues. Psychologists work on understanding and changing thoughts, behaviours and emotions using different therapies and approaches. They don't prescribe medications to help people feel better – that is done by psychiatrists.

You don't need a referral from your GP to see a counsellor or a psychologist, but your GP can help you decide if your kids would benefit from seeing someone and they can provide you with a mental health care plan. A mental health care plan will entitle your kids to Medicare rebates for up to 10 initial individual appointments with a counsellor or psychologist, depending on the type of support that is required. The Medicare rebate allows for a further 10 individual appointments if required.

Preparing to see a counsellor or a psychologist

Before you embark on organising for your kids to see a counsellor or a psychologist, it can help to find out some information such as:

1. **Why your kids are going:** have a chat with your GP about why you think your kids would benefit from meeting with a counsellor or a psychologist.
2. **Making an appointment:** will you be making the appointment or will your GP make it for you?
3. **Waiting list:** how long will your kids need to wait until you can actually get an appointment for them to see the counsellor or psychologist?
4. **Next steps:** is there anything you can do while you and your kids are waiting for the appointment?
5. **Costs and location:** how much will the appointment with the counsellor or psychologist cost? It might be expensive, so it can be a good idea to check whether your family is eligible for the Medicare rebate or, if you have it, whether this will be covered by private health insurance. And where is the counsellor located? They might work from a health centre, private consulting rooms or even from your kids' school. These days you can even do appointments online.
6. **Qualifications:** find out if your kids' counsellor or psychologist is a member of a professional organisation. And check to see if the counsellor or psychologist specialises in working with kids.

The Australian Counselling Association is a professional association representing counsellors in Australia. Their website can help you find a counsellor near you. Go to www.theaca.net.au/find-registered-counsellor.php for more help.

The Australian Psychological Society is a professional association representing psychologists in Australia. Their website can help you find a psychologist near you. Go to www.psychology.org.au/Find-a-Psychologist for more help.

YOU MENTIONED A MENTAL HEALTH CARE PLAN – WHAT IS IT AND HOW CAN I GET ONE FOR MY KIDS?

If you live in Australia, there are a few pathways which can help in making it easier to afford the cost of your kids seeing a counsellor or psychologist:

- Medicare offers a rebate for up to 20 sessions of psychological treatment. This can be face-to-face or via Zoom/telehealth if you live in a remote area.
- Private health insurers offer rebates, depending on your level of cover.

If you have a Medicare card that includes your children, they are entitled to a Medicare rebate. To access this rebate, you need to take your kids to consult with your family GP first. Your GP will assess the issues to see if your kids meet the criteria to warrant a mental health care plan. If they do, your GP will write out a mental health care plan, setting out the number of counselling or psychology sessions your kids can have that will attract the rebate. The GP will ask a few questions, fill in the plan and set goals for the visits together with you and your kids. The maximum number of rebated sessions is 20, but sometimes a GP may prescribe fewer.

A FINAL WORD ON MENTAL HEALTH

This book is all about your kids. But I want you to remember that your own health, including your mental health, is just as important. So, if reading this chapter has raised any issues of your own, do yourself and your kids a favour and speak to your GP.

If you're not quite there yet, you can access some really helpful resources that I've included for you at the end of this book, in 'Resources For You and Your Kids'.

And remember ... you've got this.

PART II
THE MEANING OF HOME FOR YOUR KIDS

'Sometimes it's the small things that matter.'

WHOEVER SAID 'home is where the heart is' got it right. It's the place where you and your loved ones can feel safe, secure and loved. Homes come in all shapes and forms, and every family is different. We understand this. We're mature adults who have lived life and experienced the ups and the downs of our own unique universe.

But what about your kids? What does home mean to them? No doubt up until now your kids have known just one version of 'home', and that's the one where you and your ex have lived together with the kids. If the definition of 'home' is about to change because you are separating, how is that going to impact their view of the future?

This part delves into the reality of changing routines, cutting out the drama and conflict, and keeping conversations flowing with your kids so they can find and accept their new definition of home. I also give you some examples of different routines you and your ex might like to consider adopting after separation, to give your children the time and space to get back to their comfort zone.

Chapter 5

WHEN AND HOW TO TALK TO YOUR KIDS ABOUT CHANGE AND CONFLICT

'Changes can be scary because it's hard to know what's around the corner. In fact, lots of us like to keep things just the way they are, even if the way they are isn't so great.'

WHY IS THIS CHANGE HAPPENING?

Separation is a major adjustment for *everyone* in your family. Change is all around you. Letting go of 'what was' and moving on to 'what is' can be a bit of a rocky road for you and for your children. Parents moving from one home to two can be overwhelming, as can other significant changes like moving to a new suburb and a new school, or adapting to new daily routines.

Kids find comfort in routine and structure, and they are often resistant to change. Remember that you and your co-parent have a lot more lead time to get used to the idea of separation because your kids are often the last to know. So, they may need some more time to get used to the changes happening around them.

Some of the big changes your children might face include:

- different day-to-day routines

- perhaps you or your ex going back to work or working different hours
- you or your ex, or perhaps both of you, moving to a new home
- having toys and personal things divided between two homes
- not having what they want, where they want it
- perhaps you or your ex living miles away instead of being close by
- being away from things that feel familiar or safe
- missing photographs or other sentimental belongings when you or your ex moves away.

While kids are becoming familiar with these changes, and especially after they have initially been told about the separation, they can question why this is all happening. In fact, rather like the 'are we there yet?' question that strikes a nerve with every parent that ever took a long, monotonous road trip, the 'why is this happening?' question can rear its head at every twist and turn of your separation journey.

HELPING YOUR KIDS COPE WITH CHANGE

Doing your best to give your kids a 'heads up' before changes happen is key to helping them adjust to their new future. The more lead time they get, the better off they'll be. Help them adjust.

If you're moving homes, explore the new neighbourhood together before the moving truck pulls up. Working at a new job? Take your kids to your new workplace or take photos and show them what you are doing and who you are working with. Spend time creating routines with your kids and have test runs before you need to rely on the routine to work smoothly.

Talk to your kids about:

- when changes will take place
- what will be different
- how life will look after the change happens
- the feelings that can accompany change.

By the way, don't forget that separation is a time of change for you too. You might be setting up a new home, dividing furniture and belongings, or starting a new job or even a new relationship. Your kids will of course notice those big changes, but they will also notice even the smallest changes.

> In around 2016 I took a call from a seriously stressed-out mum, Becky, who had recently separated from her lifelong partner, Suzanne. Becky and Suzanne had a daughter called Siobhan.
>
> Although Becky and Suzanne had not been able to reach an agreement about their property settlement, they had managed to pull together a parenting plan, and their communication about the care of Siobhan was good. Becky was calling me because she told me she needed help to finalise a property settlement. But as we began to speak, the conversation drifted to her daughter.
>
> Becky told me that although everything had been going well for Siobhan since separating, she had recently had a setback and was acting out at home. I talked to Becky about whether she had made any recent changes at home that might have impacted Siobhan. After working through a few options, Becky came to the realisation that she had very recently packed away all of the photographs that had included Suzanne from around the home.
>
> We talked about how that simple act might be impacting Siobhan, and whether she had not been as ready as Becky to make that change.

It pays to be aware of the small changes too.

Conversations to have about change

Kids often feel anxious when they don't know what to expect and they have not been prepared for a change. And too many changes at once can be overwhelming for them.

Take some time to reflect on these questions:

- What are some of the changes your children have faced in their day-to-day lives since your separation?
- How can you help your kids maintain a sense of security and stability during big changes in your family?
- What is it about your home life that you think is most important to your kids right now?
- What are some familiar things and routines that give your kids comfort and a sense of safety?
- What are some things you can keep the same?
- What are some ways you can minimise change for your children right now?

For your kids, sometimes change comes as a big surprise. And while some changes can feel exciting, others don't feel like such a good idea. Changes can be scary because it's hard to know what's around the corner. In fact, lots of us like to keep things just the way they are, even if the way they are isn't so great.

If you sense your kids' reaction to a change is that it's big or scary, talk to them about it. Together you can work out ways to make the change a little easier. Some questions that can help are:

- When we separated, what was scary for you at first?
- What changes in our family have been hard for you?
- Have there been any changes that surprised you?
- What changes have been good?
- Were there any things you were worried about at first, but then they turned out okay?
- What do you think your Mum/Dad and I can do to make changes easier for you?
- Do you have any questions or worries about other things that might change in the future?

HOW KIDS RESPOND TO CONFLICT

In around 2002, Tamara Afifi, a professor in the department of communication at the University of California, Santa Barbara, researched the impact of divorce on children. In 2017, Tamara wrote about her research, and particularly that she experienced a moment which had a huge impact on her.

She was going into families' homes and spending four to seven hours interviewing them. In one home, Tamara sat down with a 12-year-old boy and asked him about his parents' divorce. Tamara had been told by his parents that the boy was having difficulty concentrating at school. He told Tamara that his stomach often hurt. When he said his parents fought a lot, Tamara asked him if he talked to them about it. 'No,' he answered. 'Because if I bring it up, it makes the fighting worse.'

You see, parents don't always know what their kids are thinking because, like the 12-year-old boy, their kids keep their feelings to themselves. What happens next is that parents go around believing everything's okay with their kids when it's not.

Kids might suppress their emotions for lots of reasons. Perhaps they don't want to make you upset, they don't know how to express themselves, or they're just too absorbed with their grief.

Parental conflict – and in particular, when parents arguing causes a kid to feel torn between their parents – will impact how well (or not well) kids will cope after divorce. Kids who experience conflict can also experience anxiety, which can make them align with one parent over the other to ease the yucky feelings in their stomach. This can cause children to start to lose their relationship with their other parent. This is not the child's fault. It is simply their reaction to feeling caught in the conflict.

One common way that kids respond to conflict is by avoiding their feelings altogether. Kids can do this out of good intentions. They don't want their parents to feel sad or guilty. But, this means you never get to know their true feelings.

Another way kids respond to conflict is by being aggressive with others. Kids can sometimes mimic the conflict they've witnessed and lash out at you or other important people in their lives. They may not even know why they're so angry.

A third way that kids respond to conflict is to confront you or your co-parent directly. This is the most effective way for kids to deal with conflict, to tell you and your ex that they feel caught up in your arguments and to ask you to sort it out. However, it's pretty hard for kids to stand up and make these kinds of statements, and this kind of response would usually only happen with age and maturity.

As your kids reach their teenage years, they will become better at speaking openly to you and your co-parent. I hear from many parents who lament the outspoken teenagers in their midst, but isn't it better to hear directly from your kids about what is concerning them?

WHAT SHOULD YOU DO TO HELP YOUR KIDS RESPOND TO CONFLICT?

Firstly, it can help to give kids time, and then explain, and then just listen.

Try to think about and remember that you are probably on a different timetable to your children when it comes to healing from a separation. It may be that you have been grieving the end of your marriage for many months, or even years. But your kids have not. They may have been clueless about the relationship breakdown.

So, your kids might need time to mourn and accept what's happening to their family.

You could also try to give your kids enough information about the separation to reduce any uncertainty about why it happened and what will happen in the future. This doesn't mean you should sit down and have a long conversation with your kids. Instead, you could make this kind of talk flow more easily by doing another activity at the same time, like walking together or making dinner. If your kids are younger, you could play Lego together and talk then. You get the idea. When my kids were young, they used to have lots of conversations about the serious topics of their day when I was bathing them.

Secondly, try to be amicable. If your relationship allows it, do your very best to maintain as amicable a relationship as possible with your ex. Even if your co-parent speaks negatively about you, you should not engage. You see, if you refuse to argue back or say negative things in response to your co-parent, they'll probably get bored and the conflict will de-escalate.

Thirdly, it's essential that you keep a good support system. I have seen many of my clients lose what were once close social networks after divorce. This usually happens when you and your ex have had mutual friends who either drift away or take sides. As a separated parent, it's so important to have friends or family members you can share your feelings with, instead of using your kids as your mini confidantes. Work to maintain your friendships.

Encourage your kids to set up their own support networks. It can really help for them to have a friend they can confide in, especially someone who may have already been through divorce.

Don't forget to ease up on yourself, too. It's okay to be vulnerable. Your kids need to know you are human. In the end, what's most important for your kids is that they know they are loved by you and that you'll always be there for them.

TALK AND TALK MORE, AND LISTEN

Kids need to understand what's happening as their family changes. Don't avoid talking about divorce with your kids just because you don't know what to say, or you're afraid of upsetting them. The separation is already on their minds. Talking it out can be a big relief for them.

But sometimes kids just don't want to talk. I mean, you might be doing everything you can to support their feelings, but they still might find it difficult to talk to you. It might be that your kids are worried about how their feelings and actions will impact you. Kids don't want to:

- hurt your feelings
- start an argument between you and your ex

- make you angry or upset
- cause you, or their other parent, to stop seeing them
- make you feel betrayed in any way.

What's the answer in helping kids to open up to you? There's a thin line between pushing your kids to talk and encouraging them to open up. If it's been a while since you've talked about things, or if you get the sense that your kids are holding something in, just try starting a conversation. Going for a ride in the car or taking a walk with them can help. When you start your conversation with them:

- reassure your kids that it's okay to talk and ask questions
- be open to hearing what your kids have to say
- let them know that it's okay to talk to other people if they would prefer
- help your kids to think about safe adults they can turn to for advice and support. Some examples of good people for kids to turn to might be their grandparents, aunts or uncles, family friends, teachers, coaches, a counsellor or psychologist.

Being a good listener and ensuring your kids know they are truly being heard will mean more to them than you can imagine. Some tips for listening well are:

- Be careful not to put words in their mouths. But asking for clarification is okay.
- Respect their honesty. Whatever they are feeling is okay.
- Wait for your kids to finish before you respond. Try to be patient.
- It can help to calmly repeat or restate what they have said to you to acknowledge that you understand them and their feelings.
- Watch how your kids respond to how you listen, and be willing to change your approach if you sense you are losing their focus.

We all lead busy lives and there are repercussions to this. I'm pretty sure you would have no trouble recalling a time that you may have been physically involved in a conversation but still not giving your full attention to it.

In my family life, listening can easily get lost between washing the dishes and checking my phone. When your kids are speaking from the heart, make sure you put down the phone, take a breath, and really focus on what they are saying. These conversation gems can happen at the most unexpected times. Try not to miss those opportunities.

Remember, the transition through change will take some time for kids. Instead of waiting for a crisis to happen, make a habit of regularly checking in with your children to find out what's going on in their world. You could try blocking out 20 minutes a day or a couple of times a week to really touch base with them and check in on how they are feeling. Choose a time when you and your kids are free from distractions like phones, the TV and social engagements.

When you are listening to your children and getting involved in serious conversations about how they are feeling, it's helpful to resist the urge to 'fix things' or offer advice. For example, when kids are hurting or they say something that hits you hard, it can be challenging not to try to fix it right away, or to not tell them what you think, or to keep your feelings in check. But remember, what kids need most is for you to understand the problem, not necessarily to solve it then and there.

Being a good listener also means keeping your own reactions in check. Your kids need to be able to express themselves to you without worrying about how you will respond. They won't want to tell you about a sensitive issue if they expect you to blow up like a volcano and race off to save the world. Listen to what your kids are experiencing with a focused and an open mind. And when you understand accurately what they are feeling, your responses will be more in line with what they need.

CONVERSATIONS TO HAVE ABOUT TALKING

We hope our kids will always feel comfortable talking to us when they are upset. But guess what? Sometimes it's helpful for our kids to talk to someone who is not a parent. So it's important to support your kids' relationships with other trusted adults as well as their close friendships with peers. Remember, the more support, the better for your kids.

Take some time to reflect on these questions about how and who your kids are talking to:

1. Are there times when your kids are upset and they don't want to talk to you?
2. Do your kids have trusted adults they can talk to besides you and your co-parent?
3. If your kids have opened up to you, was the conversation successful and why?
4. How easy or hard is it for you to just listen to your children?
5. Are there some topics that your kids have raised with you that make you feel upset or angry or sad?
6. What could you do to become a better listener for your children?

Talking about separation and divorce isn't easy for any of us, but many kids find that once they get started, talking actually helps them feel better. Some questions that might assist you in talking to your kids about talking are:

1. Who do you talk to when you're having a hard time?
2. What grown-ups, other than me and your Mum/Dad, do you love and trust?
3. Would you feel comfortable talking to them if you are having a hard time?
4. Do you ever hold your feelings inside? How does that feel? How does it feel when you let your feelings out?
5. Do you know other kids whose parents are divorced?
6. Do you ever talk to them when you are feeling sad or angry or confused?

7. What can you say when you want us to stop what we are doing and listen to you?
8. When are some good times that you would like to talk with us, like when I'm cooking dinner or when we are driving in the car?

Separation is a major adjustment for everyone in your family. The goal is of course to get your kids and yourself through the splits as quickly and as stress-free as possible. If you can embrace and talk about change and do your best to get rid of any conflict, you're on the right path, my friend.

Oh, and don't forget to keep talking. Remember the saying 'talk is cheap'? It conjures up negative connotations, doesn't it? But I say let's flip that on its head. Talk is cheap ... and accessible and available to you and your kids. So do it and do it often.

Chapter 6

LIVING BETWEEN TWO HOMES

'It's important to take the time to get this part of your separation right, because this is your new future. This is the real deal.'

THIS IS THE REAL DEAL

The idea of living between two homes is a common one. Most separated families adopt this routine, with a goal in mind to create a peaceful and stress-free routine for their kids and for themselves.

However, to make it a positive experience for your kids to live in two homes you need to spend time preparing and planning to get it right. You want what is best for your children, and I know that you would do anything to make sure they live and grow in a safe, warm and caring situation. It's important to take the time to get this part of your separation right, because this is your new future. This is the real deal.

Separation changes the entire routine and the connections that you have probably been striving to create since the birth of your first kid. It's totally normal to feel overwhelmed or to feel like your family relationships are strained while you transition into your 'new normal'.

But it's not just about you, right? Kids may fear that losing daily contact with either you or your ex will impact their relationships. They may feel really lost about the changes to their usual routines.

To further complicate things, siblings may have differing views and concerns about the changes, which can result in a kid feeling isolated or feeling like no one, including their very own brother or sister, understands them.

I'm sorry to say that on top of all of that, just when your kids need more emotional support and time with you than they possibly ever did, you will have less energy and attention to give. Heck, you've just been on the rollercoaster of a lifetime and you are in urgent need of a holiday somewhere warm, sunny and sandy. You find yourself in a battle of needs, reality, stress and adjustment.

It's not easy to work out all the pieces of this puzzle on your own. Do yourself a favour and reach out to your support network, your best mate, your family, your psychologist, your family lawyer to help you figure out what the plan for living between two homes is going to look like for your unique family situation.

If you can, and the relationship allows it, take some time to talk with your ex about how the two-home idea is going to work for each of you. Consider the following questions:

- What support will each of you need to be a good parent in each of your homes?
- How do you each differ in your parenting styles?
- Does it really matter if you each do things differently? If so, what are each of you willing to change?
- How will you communicate with each other about the kids?
- How are you both going to manage the kids' expectations, wants and needs?
- What is the best plan for the children right now?

HELPING YOUR KIDS TO ADJUST

Sometimes it's the small things that matter.

You have enormous power to help your kids cope with change, even as you too are adjusting and coping with change. Over time, you and your co-parent will be guiding your little humans towards a new sense of normal in their two-home family. This can all be helped in small ways – your words, your body language, your sense of calm all help your kids to accept their new normal, and this allows them space to grow into their new routine.

But it's not just the small things that will give your kids space to grow. It's the big things too. Working to manage your emotions and freeing your kids from conflict can make a big difference to them. Whether you have already separated or are thinking about separation and are finding yourself in difficult situations with your ex, showing your kids how to use healthy coping strategies for handling stress, strong feelings and difficult changes by doing those things yourself will also help your kids to grow successfully into their new life in two homes.

Probably the most important thing that kids need to grow into and accept their new two-home family is time. They need time to build trust that their new home situation is stable and secure. They need time to build trust that their relationship with you and their other parent is also stable and secure. So, take things carefully. Build slowly and methodically on your kids' routines, changeovers and time spent with your co-parent.

MAKING YOUR RULES AND EXPECTATIONS CLEAR

Even under the best circumstances, moving back and forth between two homes can be confusing and unsettling for kids. It can feel like moving between two very different worlds, and this is especially so if you and your co-parent tend to do things differently.

When kids are stressed out, they can act out their frustrations by:

- acting younger than their age
- sulking
- withdrawing into themselves
- throwing temper tantrums or having meltdowns
- deliberately leaving things they need at your co-parent's home

- being disrespectful
- pushing limits
- becoming clingy
- being hyper or overly fearful.

Try to pay attention to what's going on in your home when your kids are moving back and forth. Think about what you can do to make the change easier for your children.

One of the best things you can do is to have clear rules and expectations in place. This kind of predictability will help your kids to feel secure when they are living with you.

For example, if your kids know what to expect during transitions, they will feel more relaxed and have less anxiety. Normal everyday life is already pretty hectic for your kids. Add two homes and two parents' schedules into the mix and it's very easy to see how children might feel overwhelmed or confused about moving between two homes. You can help by keeping things as predictable and uncomplicated as possible.

Two homes can mean two very different lives for kids. There can be different rules about screen time and bedtime, or what is considered appropriate language and clothing. It can be a pretty tough challenge for kids to continually shift between different rules and expectations.

Of course, if it's all smooth sailing and you and your co-parent are on the same page about rules, everyday routines and structure then you've got this challenge sorted. I mean, that would be happy days. But, good co-parenting doesn't mean you have to do everything exactly the same.

If you and your co-parent don't exactly see eye to eye, don't focus on that negative. Focus on the core values such as safety, education, respect and health. Try to reach common ground in those areas. Try not to argue over parenting styles for the other bits and pieces like bedtimes, food choices, how homework gets done and how much TV kids watch. Sure, in a perfect world your kids would transition seamlessly in and out of the same rules and expectations in each home. But if that's not doable, and inevitably it won't be, try not to stress the small stuff. It's understandable that you might feel very upset that your co-parent is allowing your 10-year-old to stay up to 11 o'clock on a Friday night, but as long as said 10-year-old is well fed and loved, and is not being impacted, let it be. And if you do have concerns, always gently raise those concerns with your co-parent before escalating. There just might an opportunity to positively influence the situation.

GIVE YOUR KIDS A CALENDAR

Empowering your kids by giving them a clear pathway forward is a game changer. The easiest way to do this is to give your kids access to a family calendar.

Grab a big bright wall calendar and hang it in an area of your home that the kids can easily access, like the kitchen, the loungeroom or even right by the front door. It doesn't really matter where, as long as the kids can see it every day and update it regularly.

Invite your kids to choose a colour for each home to help them keep track of their time with you and your co-parent. Mark important dates like family birthdays (yes, all of them, including your co-parent's birthday), school events, holidays and other special occasions. For older or more tech-savvy kids, create a shared online calendar or a calendar on their phone or device.

Work to keep the schedule predictable, and make sure the kids always have access to it.

It also helps to ask kids about how they feel about their schedule. Although it may not be possible to change the schedule, knowing how your kids feel can give you a chance to make changes where possible, or at least explain why you can't make changes.

It's also important to be flexible. Giving your kids choices and a voice is important for them. This is especially so when there is so little they control. Try to be flexible about arrangements or schedule changes if that will benefit your kids and keep their lives more comfortable.

Julie was a client whose sporty, outgoing 12-year-old daughter, Sophie, kept missing every second netball game, which were played on Saturdays. This occurred because the agreement in place was that Sophie would spend every second weekend, from Friday night to Sunday night, with her dad, Rob. The problem was that Rob lived two hours away, and Julie and Rob agreed that it wasn't in their daughter's best interests to sit in a car for long periods of time over one day just to make it to a netball game.

But Sophie really loved netball. And she didn't want to miss her games. You can probably guess what happened next. Sophie started to say that she didn't want to go to Rob's home. She started to make excuses that Julie accepted, and this had a terrible impact on her relationship with her dad. Sophie was making big choices for herself.

Julie was in a bind because all she wanted to do was ensure that Sophie was happy.

Julie and Rob came up with a flexible workaround. During the netball season, Sophie spent every Friday night with Julie and Rob picked up Sophie at netball on Saturday. Instead of heading back to her mum's house on Sunday night, Sophie then spent the Sunday night with her dad and was driven to school by him on Monday morning.

This flexible solution worked for Julie and Rob and ensured that Sophie didn't have to choose. Asking a kid which parent they want to be with can create stress and divided loyalty, especially with younger children. Your kids love both parents, and saying yes to one parent means saying no to the other. You should make the big decisions, while giving your kids the opportunity to make some of the smaller ones.

GET BACK TO CALM AND CARRY ON BY HELPING YOUR KIDS CREATE RITUALS

You're superhuman if you are a parent. Seriously. You glide through hundreds of changes in your week without so much as batting an eye.

Rachael wakes up with a fever so you change your schedule, make a few calls and work from home to be with her. Brad gives you late notice about soccer practice and the dinner you had planned magically turns into takeaway from the local roast chicken shop. Sure, some of those changes are stressful, but you pretty much have the power to roll with the punches.

Kids, on the other hand, don't find living life on the fly as easy. This is accentuated when kids live across two homes. Two homes involves juggling a schedule that may not always be predictable. It involves dealing with different parenting styles, different rules, different places, different people and different ways of being a family.

On top of dealing with all those differences, moving back and forth between houses has the very real potential to create some serious emotional stress for kids. This can play out in many different ways.

> I remember a client of mine, a young mum to a six-year-old boy called Joey, telling me that each time Joey came back from his dad's home he was bouncing off the walls and testing limits. Joey's mum was aware that when Joey was at his dad's, he spent a good deal of his time playing on the computer while his dad worked. Joey's mum was beside herself with worry about how best to handle this situation, and she had started to think that it might be best if Joey stopped spending time with his dad. You see, Joey's mum was stuck picking up the pieces and getting life back on track. The worst part was that it started all over again the next time Joey went to spend time with his dad.

In this example, Joey's mum wasn't really sure about whether the father's approach to parenting was the cause of Joey's negative behaviours when he returned to her. Joey's mum had tried to have conversations with the father to figure out how to fix things but they just weren't able to get anywhere with those conversations.

If you're tired of going through the same old reactions when your kids come back, there is a simple strategy you can use to get back to calm and carry on.

Creating a Regulation Transition Routine

To ease the stress of going back and forth, try creating a Regulation Transition Routine (or RTR) for your kids. A RTR involves creating a structured and predictable environment for your children every time they enter or leave your home. This involves doing an activity with your kids, or giving them the space to do the activity on their own, when they leave or come back to your home. The beauty of implementing a RTR is that it works for all ages.

Let me show you.

To get started, it's best to pick an activity that fits your kid's personality and age. A child who is quiet or laid-back might want to read a book. Or if they are younger, to work on a colouring book. A kid who is more active or outgoing might like to play outside. Or if they are older, take the dog for a walk.

Ask your kids what they would like to do when they return to your home.

Ideas for younger kids include:

- reading a book together in a cosy place
- sitting and playing a game or watching a TV show
- riding bikes or playing with a ball
- colouring or drawing a picture
- playing with Play-Doh.

Ideas for older kids include:

- going for a walk together
- heading to the local café or takeaway shop
- checking out YouTube or other social feeds
- reading in a quiet corner
- phoning a friend for a chat
- cooking dinner together.

Thinking back to my example of Joey. One way that Joey's mum could help Joey is by choosing an activity they could do together as soon as he walks through the door. Perhaps Joey loves to colour and draw. When Joey arrives, he and his mum could spend 20 minutes colouring together. They could chat about Joey's time with his dad and what the following period of time will look like with his mum. Joey has a chance to decompress, and his mum has a way to help Joey transition into their routine.

By making each transition predictable, you give your kids the emotional space they need to shift gears between the two households. A RTR helps your kids feel less stressed because they'll know what to expect when they walk through your door.

MAKE EACH HOUSE A HOME AND FILL EACH HOME WITH LOVE

Remember, the two homes may be quite different. You may be working with a much larger budget than your co-parent, or vice versa. Your co-parent may have more toys or electronics in their home. But what kids want most is a home filled with love and support. They want a place where they can relax and feel secure. And we know kids do better when they feel a sense of belonging in both homes.

Even if your kids don't spend equal time in each home, you can still make your place feel like a home. Make a special space where the kids can keep their things when they are with you.

Remember though, special doesn't mean expensive or large. If finances are tight, try to be creative. Think about what will help your kids feel comfortable. Some ideas to get you thinking are:

- Buy a cabinet or find an old small cupboard. Paint or decorate it in your kids' favourite colours and have it in their bedroom or in an area of the home that they frequently use. Invite your kids to keep their special things in the cupboard or perhaps turn it into a place to store fun activities like arts and craft or colouring.
- Pick out photos your kids like (not just photos of you with the kids) that they can put in their room or on a shelf.

- Have everyday things your kids use and need – like pyjamas, favourite toys, toothbrushes and clothes – in each home so that kids don't need to worry about carrying stuff back and forth.
- Keep things in your home that support a hobby or an interest that your kids enjoy.

Remember, what matters most to your children is that your home feels like a place where they belong. The majority of separated families adopt a routine of living in two homes with a goal to create a peaceful and stress-free routine for their kids and for themselves. But to get to this nirvana takes time preparing and planning.

Chapter 7

NESTING: THE HOW, WHY, WHERE AND WHEN

'Clear and calm communication is crucial.'

WHAT IS NESTING?

Does the traditional 'two home' approach in which the kids have to move between two homes have to be the default scenario? Absolutely not.

'Nesting' (or 'bird nesting') means that the kids stay in the family home after the divorce while you and your co-parent move in and out to care for them. Just like birds alighting from the nest. The motivating concept behind nesting is that there is less disruption for the kids. Their environment and routine stay somewhat the same.

We all know that getting divorced is tough, especially if you have kids. And even if the decision to separate is the best, or only, decision for you, the actual separation can be traumatising for kids. I'm not going to sugar-coat that for you. But, research has shown the best way to avoid risking the wellbeing of your children is to keep the separation process as low-conflict and amicable as possible.

Easier said than done, right?

Well, perhaps nesting is your solution. Ask yourself this question: will keeping the family home intact – where you and your co-parent rotate living with your kids, while otherwise living in separate residences – work for you?

Nesting means that it's not just the kids who don't have to move back and forth between two homes. It also means the following do not need to move back and forth, or need to be duplicated in a second home:

- your kids' personal possessions, toys and books
- clothing and toiletries
- school materials, homework, and sport and music equipment
- furniture, electronics, food and other supplies
- the much loved family pet.

When a separated family are nesting, there is just one version of each of these things, in one home. This saves significantly on the cost of duplicating essential items in a second home.

Nesting can also mean less stress for your kids. Why? It's simple really. The kids don't have to worry about keeping track of their things because they're not moving between two places. They don't have to concern themselves about packing bags and dealing with situations where they have forgotten something.

This living arrangement can help give your kids more consistency and continuity in their lives. I've learned from speaking to many separated parents over the years that nesting can help in the early days of a separation, before you've had the time or mind space to figure out what's going to happen next. The families I have worked with who decide to try nesting have created their own variations of nesting arrangements, being creative in finding what works best for their individual family.

THINGS TO CONSIDER

This solution may be a short-term one for your family. But as with most things in life, there are pros and cons to consider, and I will take you through those now.

A simpler arrangement

There are many positives to this arrangement.

> Jane, who lived in a nesting situation for six months with her kids, then aged 6 and 10, and their dad, says that her kids didn't really notice the separation during that phase. The more difficult time was after the nesting period, when the kids were transitioning back and forth between the two separate homes. But Jane found that the time spent nesting gave her the opportunity to carefully plan her next move, and it took the pressure off having to make quick decisions about the living arrangements for her and the kids.

For lots of kids of separated parents, the shifting back and forth between homes can be challenging, both practically and emotionally. Kids forget toys, homework, sports uniforms. Combining this with the challenge of different spaces, different routines and different rules can be hard for them. A nesting arrangement removes the complexities of moving your kids between two homes.

A more affordable arrangement

Financially there can be positives. Keeping two homes large enough for kids, close to school and other activities, and duplicating clothes, toiletries and furniture, can be expensive. This can be especially difficult if you and your co-parent have not finalised a property settlement, or are having difficulties agreeing who pays those expenses.

A smaller, modestly furnished second home, or 'bolt hole' that parents can share, can be a cheaper option in the short term. Alternatively, moving to another family member's home or a good friend's home can also help you reduce costs when you are nesting.

Short-term nesting is usually best

I've seen nesting work out well for clients who have separated amicably, but only if it's done on a short-term basis. Never have I seen nesting go on forever. In reality, the uncertainty of not knowing what it will really be like to have separate homes can be confusing for kids.

> A family that I worked with nested for the remainder of their teenager's senior year in high school (which was a period of around three months) to keep her grounded and in her usual routine. The parents had a very amicable divorce: they both wanted to end the marriage and were committed to putting their daughter's interests ahead of their own.

Dr Fran Walfish, a family and relationship psychotherapist and author of *The Self-Aware Parent: Resolving conflict and building a better bond with your child*, agrees that a short-term nesting plan is best, and finds that the method is beneficial to kids.

Dr Walfish says that the shock of the separation for kids can be softened by a brief transitional period where the kids' home environment remains the same and the only change is the presence of one parent or the other. She believes that any longer than around three months of nesting risks giving the kids an inaccurate message that you and your co-parent are working on reconciliation.

It is common for kids to fantasise and wish for their parents to work things out and become one family unit again. So, it's important to be very clear with your kids, if they are old enough to understand, that you and your co-parent have separated and that the nesting arrangement is short term.

You need to be amicable to make nesting work

If you and your ex have difficulties communicating, or if there is family violence that has occurred in your relationship, nesting is not for you. You need to have good communication, feel safe and be amicable with your co-parent. Otherwise, nesting can create an opportunity for the very kind of conflict that you are trying to avoid.

Imagine this scenario. It's your week with the kids in the family home. You decide to make a big, yummy pot of bolognaise sauce and you use the last of the garlic. You don't have time to go to the shops to replace the garlic. When your co-parent moves back into the family home for their week with the kids, they decide to make a dish that needs garlic. When they express frustration that there is no garlic available, the kids casually mention that you made a big pot of bolognaise sauce and used garlic the previous week. Your co-parent then calls you and tells you how self-centred you are for having used the last of the garlic and not replacing it.

It's a pretty benign example, but imagine if the issue was a bigger one. Imagine this. Your co-parent's new partner spends time at the family home and leaves their underwear there. How are you likely to respond when you find the underwear of your ex's new squeeze?

You see, sharing a home can create many opportunities for parents to trigger one another, which will not benefit the kids. You need to go into the process with eyes wide open. You need to have good communication and be amicable to make nesting work.

PRACTICAL THINGS TO CONSIDER ABOUT NESTING

You need to view the nest as the kids' home. It's no longer the family home. It's not 'yours' or 'ours'. It's the kids' home. So, when you find yourself in the scenario where the floors need to be swept, the toilet needs cleaning and the lawn needs to be mown, try not to feel resentful that your co-parent hasn't done those jobs. Just do it because it needs to be done for your kids, in their home. Alternatively, organise a cleaner to come to the house.

Having a clear and detailed written plan about how costs will be shared in the kids' home is a game changer. Work out who is responsible for what, including meeting the costs of utilities, groceries, gardening, maintenance and repairs. Who is going to pay the bills? Is everything split 50/50, or will the expenses be weighted differently based on each of your financial circumstances? You could consider opening a joint bank account specifically for running the kids' home.

Clear and calm communication is crucial. It's a good idea to have regular check-ins with your co-parent and also between the kids and your co-parent. You can formalise these check-ins if it helps, perhaps with a set day each month to catch up and discuss any issues or whether anything needs tweaking. You could also try hanging a 'communication board' in a prominent place or using a parenting app so you can all (including your kids) track what's going on and what's coming up.

Keep the rules in the nest consistent. No-one should get to be the 'fun parent', leaving the other to do the hard, everyday stuff. Agree to the rules and write them down in a co-parenting agreement. Agree to review it regularly.

If possible, you should each have a private space in the nest. This is where you can keep some of your private things. It's important that you both respect that space.

Regarding possible dating, bringing new partners into the nest can be very confusing for kids and upsetting for the other parent. It's a good idea to adopt a 'no dates in the nest' policy and keep your dating outside the kids' home.

You need to be clear about handover in the nest. Think about choosing midday rather than the beginning of the day when everyone is rushing to get to school and work, or the end of the day when everyone is tired and hungry.

Importantly, keep the nest as clear of conflict as possible. The nest is your kids' safe haven. However, when conflict arises, work to find amicable solutions.

Remember, nesting can be a great transitional situation for your kids, but it's not without challenges. Remaining in the 'family home' can trigger emotions from past events and this can be difficult when everyone is trying to navigate a new life. If you and your co-parent are on the same page about nesting, trial it and see how it goes. If it gets too hard, plan out the next steps and move forward slowly and carefully.

WHAT IF NESTING IS NOT AN OPTION FOR YOU?

Even if you think that nesting sounds fabulous, it's not always a suitable plan.

Money is key. You and your co-parent need to be able to afford to continue to maintain the family home and to also maintain a short-term lease arrangement for the bolt hole if you are not going to live away in other people's homes.

You also need a supremely calm and committed attitude that might be reflective of Gwyneth Paltrow and Chris Martin in their 'conscious uncoupling' co-parenting arrangements. But it can be hard to reach this level of commitment if your separation has been rough or your ex is just difficult.

If nesting is not an option for you and you need to adopt a 'two home' plan, try these five ideas:

- **As much as possible, keep the general structure and routine the same in both homes.** Try to keep the same bedtime, mealtimes, wakeup time, homework schedule and extracurricular activities for your kids. The more stable their lives are, the less separation anxiety your kids will suffer. If you can't keep the same routines and structures, at least try to be aware of what's going on in the other home and make allowances for that.
- **As much as possible, keep rules, expectations, and consequences the same in both homes.** If you can do this effectively, you will see a reduction in angry behaviour and emotional problems with your teenagers.
- **If possible, keep school the same. It's not a good idea to change your kids' home and their school at the same time as separating.** Losing the continuity of the same friends, teachers and school playground could negatively impact your children, who are already dealing with the separation shakeup.
- **Nurture, nourish and facilitate relationships for your kids with their extended family.** When parents divorce, sometimes kids lose access to their cousins, aunts and uncles. The more people who love and care about your kids, the less painful the separation will be for them. Let your kids be loved and cared for by lots of people. Remember, it takes a village to raise a child.

- **Never argue or give the silent treatment with your co-parent in front of the kids.** This kind of behaviour makes it difficult for kids to continue to have a loving and respectful relationship with both parents. And it's the number one complaint from children of divorced parents.

* * *

Nesting can absolutely be a positive experience if it's right for your family. Nesting can mean less disruption, but only if you have a co-parent who is on the same page as you and there is a healthy dose of respect between you. Nesting is not a long-time solution – keep this in mind when you are considering what to do next on your separation journey.

Chapter 8

WHAT ABOUT NEW PEOPLE COMING INTO THE HOME?

'Tread carefully and take your time.'

YOU MAY BE READY, BUT ARE YOUR KIDS?

The dust has settled. The kids are doing fine, and you've got your mojo back.

Dating or starting a new relationship may feel like an exciting new chapter in your life, but your kids may have a very different view. For your kids, seeing Mum or Dad out and about and spending time with someone different may stir up lots of confusing and uncomfortable feelings. It can also serve as another reminder that their life won't ever go back to the way it was before.

Introducing a new partner to your children

One of the most common questions my clients ask me is, 'When should I be introducing a new partner to my children?' My usual answer is to take your time and don't introduce a new partner to your kids if you are dating casually. Give new relationships time to grow into something more serious before involving your kids. It's a-okay to let your kids know you are seeing someone. They might be curious and have questions that you should answer as honestly as possible.

But involving your kids too soon can backfire. There doesn't need to be a meeting until you are in a more serious relationship. When kids form a relationship with a parent's new boyfriend or girlfriend and it doesn't work out, it can trigger the same sense of loss they felt when the separation happened.

Don't do it to them.

When the time is right and you are ready to introduce your children to your new partner, try doing something your kids will enjoy that also gives them some space to get to know your new partner. Meeting in an informal setting may help your kids feel more relaxed. It could be at a local park, at the movies, at your local pizza restaurant or a trip to the zoo.

Rather than planning a long visit, keep the meeting brief and casual. Keep your expectations realistic, and don't pressure your children to give you their opinions on the new person. Instead, give them the opportunity to get to know each other.

The age of your children is a factor that you will definitely want to take into consideration. Younger kids may feel confused, angry or sad because they can feel possessive of their parents and the life that you have all been enjoying. Constance Ahrons, Ph.D, conducted a 20-year study of 173 children of divorce and concluded that most children find their parent's new relationship behaviours confusing and strange.

On the other hand, older kids can be more accepting of your new partner, but they may still see that person as a threat to their relationships with you. Dr Ahrons also found that teenagers can find open affection between their parent and a partner concerning, so it can be helpful to go easy on physical contact in front of them.

By building new relationships thoughtfully, you have the opportunity to model those positive behaviours for your kids. This can have a positive impact on how your kids then view relationships in the future.

In the early stages of a new relationship, it's important for you to stay in charge of discipline and significant parenting decisions. If your new partner becomes a disciplinarian too early in the game, kids may come to resent them. This can create long-lasting tensions between your new partner and your kids.

As your kids' relationship with your partner grows, your partner can transition into being more of a parental authority in your kids' lives.

Following a separation, kids may worry that you love your new partner more than you love them. While you may be really excited to be in a new relationship, be mindful that your kids still need one-on-one time with you and reassurance about their importance in your life.

Make sure you are careful about sleepovers with your new partner when your children are living with you. It's never a good idea to plan an overnight stay in your home right away because it can cause rivalry between your new partner and your kids.

If you co-parent, you should have plenty of opportunities to spend overnight time with your new partner when your kids are with your co-parent. Having your new partner spend overnight time when the kids are around should only be an option once you are sure that your relationship is tracking to a permanent arrangement.

Five tips for introducing your new partner to your kids

Here are five tips for introducing your new partner to your kids:

1. **Careful timing is essential.** Kids need time to adjust, and it can take a year or two for them to get over their anger, sadness and other emotions that they experienced during your separation. So, if you introduce your kids to someone you are dating casually, this may complicate their adjustment to your separation. Tread carefully and take your time.
2. **Your kids may see your new partner as a rival.** Just because you think you've fallen in love, it doesn't mean that your kids will share your positive feelings. Be prepared for some backlash, and remember to remind your children how much you love them.
3. **Consider their need for security and reassurance.** Introducing a new partner to your kids too soon can increase stress in your home and halt your kids' journey in coming to terms with the separation. Give your kids lots of reassurance that you have plenty of love to go around and you will always be present in their lives.

4. **Ask yourself if your new partner is a good fit.** You may have great chemistry with your new partner. But ask yourself if they are a good fit for your *family*. Then put your big-person pants on and make the best decision for you and your kids.
5. **Get your kids involved in how they would like to meet your new partner for the first time.** Picture this. You've been dating someone for a while and feel relatively confident that you are heading towards commitment. The next best step is to talk to your kids and explain that you are dating someone who you care about and you'd like to introduce them. Ask your kids if they have any questions. Keep the first meeting short and low key. Go to a neutral spot for the first meeting. Ask your kids where they'd like to go, and don't invite your new partner's children to join you on the first few visits.

SHARING THE NEWS WITH YOUR EX

It's a good idea to make sure that when big changes are happening in your life, you take responsibility for informing your co-parent instead of expecting your kids to deliver the news. Some examples of big changes that can occur for you include having a new boyfriend or girlfriend and wanting to introduce the kids, deciding to remarry, or even expecting another child.

While you may think it's none of your co-parent's business, informing them in advance of big changes spares your kids from walking on eggshells, being pumped for information or being upset by your ex's unexpected reaction.

IF YOUR EX RE-PARTNERS

Kids can be fiercely loyal to their parents, and they may feel like they are betraying one parent by liking the other parent's new partner.

If you find yourself in the situation where your co-parent is the one who has re-partnered, help put your kids at ease by reassuring them that it's okay for them to like or even love this new person. If this feels difficult, at least work hard at resisting the urge to make negative comments about the new partner. If you can do this, you are doing your kids a favour.

> A couple of years ago I met a doting dad, Geoffrey, whose nine-year-old son, Kyle, spent equal time with his parents. My first meeting with Geoffrey involved a conversation about Kyle's mum, who had recently re-partnered. Geoffrey told me that Kyle had cried when he found out his Mum had a new boyfriend, and that he felt really awkward when this new person came to dinner.
>
> Kyle eventually confided to Geoffrey that he was worried that he would be betraying his Dad if he liked his Mum's new boyfriend.
>
> Geoffrey was a switched-on dad who knew that Kyle's best interests were the most important thing, and he needed to set his feelings aside. Geoffrey told Kyle that it was okay to like his Mum's new boyfriend.

Geoffrey and Kyle's story exemplifies the importance of keeping your kids' interests at the forefront of your mind, always.

Remind your kids that they will always have their parents. Kids need to know that Mum will always be their mum and Dad will always be their dad, no matter who else comes into the picture. Parents don't get replaced.

* * *

If you have met someone new then I am very happy for you and wish you the best in this new chapter in your life. Just remember to take it slowly to give your kids time to catch up and to adjust to the relationship. And if it's your ex who has moved on, do your best to assure your kids that their other parent will always love them and that you will always be there for them.

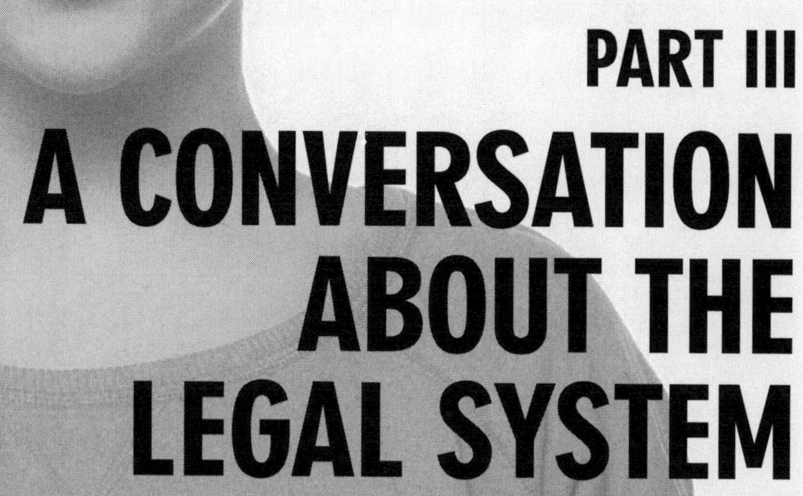

PART III

A CONVERSATION ABOUT THE LEGAL SYSTEM

'I want you to know what going to court means so that you can make informed decisions about how the outcome of your separation can be best managed.'

GOING THROUGH A SEPARATION and going to court are two very different prospects. Just because you and your ex are separating does not mean that you will be involved in court proceedings, and my greatest wish for your family is that you never set foot in a courtroom. There are lots of ways to ensure that your separation remains on an amicable pathway so you can avoid court.

I implore you to research how your family can follow a peaceful process, for the sake of your kids. For starters, finding a family lawyer who understands the benefits of keeping your family out of court will help immensely. And there are plenty of us around. Do your research and take time to find a family lawyer whose values resonate with yours.

But sadly, there are situations where the rose-coloured glasses may need to be removed and you will find yourself in court. This can be for many reasons, and not necessarily of your choosing.

I have written this part to guide you about how the family law legal system works in Australia and how to talk to your children about court. Do us both a favour and do not skip this part. Read it from start to finish, and then read it again. Why? Because I want you to be aware of what may lie just around the corner. I want you to know what going to court means so you can make informed decisions about how the outcome of your separation can be best managed.

Chapter 9

SUCCESSFULLY NAVIGATING THE LEGAL SYSTEM

'If you are in court, you are essentially asking a judge to make a decision about the future care and wellbeing of your kids.'

It is my greatest wish for you that you are in a situation where you and your co-parent can work together to figure out the best way to manage the care of your kids.

But sadly, the nirvana of conscious uncoupling (thanks for sharing, Gwyneth Paltrow and Chris Martin) is not attainable for everyone.

There are so many reasons why you may find yourself walking into court to get assistance in determining an outcome for the future care and wellbeing of your kids. Some of the most common reasons are:

- your ex isn't interested in attending mediation with you to discuss the care of the kids
- there are issues of family violence and/or abuse that are impacting you and/or your kids
- you can't talk reasonably with your ex and you can't reach an agreement
- your ex has commenced proceedings

- you want to move away with the kids and your ex does not agree to the move.

These are just some of the reasons that you might find yourself in court.

HOW THE LAW RELATES TO YOUR KIDS IN AUSTRALIA

If you are in court, you are essentially asking a judge to make a decision about the future care and wellbeing of your kids. Now there are always opportunities to negotiate along the way, and if appropriate for your circumstances, you should be active in those negotiations, with a view to getting out of the system as quickly as possible. In fact, the family law system in Australia actively encourages families to agree on parenting arrangements without going to, or staying in, court.

But, if you find yourself hitting brick walls and negotiations are not on the cards, you'll need to hold on for the ride.

The *Family Law Act 1975*, which has been updated along the way, is the legislation that helps the court determine how your kids will be cared for in the future. (From now on, when I refer to the *Family Law Act 1975*, I'll simply call it the Act.) The Act focuses on the rights of children and the responsibilities that each parent has towards them. And here's a lightbulb moment for you ... what the Act does not do is focus on a parent's rights. It's all about the kids and their best interests. Keep that little nugget in your back pocket, and if you have to, pull it out to remind your ex that it's not about you two. Not at all. The Act aims to ensure children can enjoy a meaningful relationship with each of their parents, and that they're also protected from harm.

Now there are of course other reasons, besides your kids, that you may be in court. Family law in Australia refers to legal matters relating to marriage, divorce, separation, parenting arrangements, property, child support, spousal maintenance and adoption. But I'm not going to spend time going into those areas in this book because this book is focused on your kids.

The Act states that children have a right to a meaningful relationship with both parents. However, there is also a requirement that you and your co-parent must fulfill your duties and meet your responsibilities concerning the care, welfare and development of your kids. This includes financial support.

If the court is asked to decide about a parenting matter, the Act says that the best interests of the kids will be paramount. The Act says that when determining what is in the kids' best interests, we need to consider the following:

1. The benefit to the children of having a meaningful relationship with both you and your co-parent.
2. The need to protect the kids from physical or psychological harm by being exposed to abuse, neglect or family violence.

The Act says that point 2 above is more important than point 1.

There's a long list of additional considerations, including any views expressed by the kids. But the weight given to each of these additional considerations varies and depends on your family's circumstances and the age of your kids.

WHAT IS 'PARENTAL RESPONSIBILITY' AND DO I HAVE IT?

You may have heard the term 'parental responsibility' talked about by other parents who have separated, or even mentioned by your family lawyer. What is it?

In a nutshell, it means all the duties, powers, responsibilities and authority that you and your co-parent have in relation to your kids.

If there are no orders about parental responsibility, you and your co-parent each have parental responsibility for your kids. This means that both of you can make decisions about the kids, independently from each other.

If you and your co-parent would like to create a legal obligation to make joint decisions about major long-term issues (like your kids' health, education, religion, name), you should enter into an order for equal shared parental responsibility.

If you don't want to create that obligation but would like both of you to have equal parental responsibility, you could either make no order about parental responsibility, or make an order for each of you to retain parental responsibility.

Or, if you want to transfer parental responsibility to you alone, or allocate just some aspects of parental responsibility to yourself (like, for example, what schools your kids will attend), and you and your co-parent agree, you can make that order.

UNDERSTANDING THE COURT PROCESS

In my years of experience, families can wait between 12 months and three years to have final orders made in their matters. Of course, some cases do settle more quickly. However, if your matter can't be resolved by agreement, there's usually no way to fast track the final hearing.

Let's talk about the court process. I don't plan to go into great detail about the rules and regulations (that would be a whole book in itself), but I do want to give you a helpful overview so that you are aware of, and ready for, the steps to take.

While you're reading this chapter, keep in mind that once the court process commences, you can continue to negotiate. Yep, that's right. You can cut and run at any time, my friend. If an agreement can be reached between you and your ex, a consent order can be filed and the matter will be finalised. This can be done at any time. And make no mistake, an early exit from the court process will save you time, money and - most importantly - your sanity. You'll also most likely get a thumbs up from the judge too.

Now on to the court process. Grab a tea or coffee, or perhaps something slightly stronger, and imagine you, your ex and your kids walking through these next steps during what is already a stressful time in your life.

Before you go to court

There are certain procedures that you, your ex and your lawyer need to use to attempt to resolve your dispute, or to otherwise try to narrow the issues in dispute, so that your matter can be resolved outside of court if possible.

The court requires you to complete some specific pre-action procedures:

- participating in dispute resolution, such as mediation
- writing to your ex and setting out your position and including a genuine offer to resolve your dispute
- giving your ex your disclosure documents (which is more related to financial matters).

The idea behind the pre-action procedures is to encourage you and your ex to exchange information and at least understand each other's position. These procedures can help to resolve your issues, and even avoid court.

Sometimes it's not viable to go through the pre-action procedures. Some examples of this include:

- your matter is urgent or there are allegations of family violence and/or child abuse
- situations where your ex simple refuses to negotiate
- a time limit is close to expiring. For example, if it is close to being 12 months since your divorce order was made (where you must have reached a property settlement within 12 months of being divorced) there may not be sufficient time to work through the pre-action procedures.

It's important to give pre-action procedures a genuine attempt. If you don't, and you don't have a reasonable reason like those listed above, the court may order that you or your ex (whoever was not playing ball) pay all or part of the other person's legal costs. The court can also take the non-compliance into account when making orders. *Yikes.* Don't let that happen to you.

Starting the court process

An application to commence court proceedings needs the following documents to be filed at court:

- **An Initiating Application:** this document sets out the orders you want the court to make on an interim (short term) and final (long term) basis.
- **An Affidavit:** this document is your story. It should set out the relevant facts and circumstances, and forms the background for your application.
- **A Notice of Child Abuse, Family Violence or Risk:** this document sets out any concerns relating to any risk to your kids or allegations of family violence. Even if these are not issues in your matter, you are still required to complete this document.
- **A Financial Statement (if your matter includes financial issues):** this document sets out your income, expenses, assets, liabilities and financial resources.

Once your application has been filed and 'sealed' by the court, it needs to be personally served on your ex or their lawyer. Your ex must then file a Response to the Initiating Application and the other documents listed above.

Once court proceedings have started, and you and your ex have both set out what you want to happen in relation to the care and wellbeing of your kids, you should still attempt to negotiate.

Your first court appearance

You and your ex will both be required to attend the first court event. If you are self-represented, you will need to be ready to tell the judge what orders you want them to make. If you have a family lawyer, be guided by their advice to you.

(I understand that you may be in a situation where you cannot afford a family lawyer or perhaps you might be thinking that you can have a go at running your court matter on your own. In my experience it can cause problems down the track if you are self-represented and are not confident in the steps you should be taking. This can result in your position not being put clearly to the court about what orders you are seeking or missing the inclusion of important and relevant evidence. But even more importantly, it can be very difficult to remain clear headed and to make decisions about your case when you are so emotionally invested. If you do decide to represent yourself, I suggest, at the very least, that you consult with a family lawyer up front to find out about your legal rights and get some information about how you should proceed.)

During the COVID-19 pandemic, most court events have been done using virtual meeting spaces via Microsoft Teams (similar to Zoom), with only very limited face-to-face court appearances. There have been many benefits to this change, including reduced costs. But it can be difficult to negotiate when you are not physically in court. I'm not sure whether some court events will stay virtual. Time will tell whether this move into a new world of saved time and costs will stay with us.

The first court event usually rolls like this:

1. The judge will determine any application for interim orders sought (if there is time, otherwise the judge will set the matter down for an interim hearing on another day). The judge will want an indication of the following: a summary of the relevant facts and issues in dispute, the evidence and the witnesses who would be called to give evidence, and the expected duration of the trial.
2. The judge will also make directions as to how the matter will go along. Examples of directions are:
   - that you and your ex attend private mediation
   - whether you and your ex attend a child inclusive conference and/or a child dispute conference
   - that you and your ex exchange any relevant disclosure documents

- whether it is necessary to appoint an Independent Children's Lawyer
- whether a Family Report needs to be prepared
- any specific directions sought by either you or your ex, such as drug testing, medical reports or psychiatric assessments.

Depending on how your matter goes, you may be required to go back to court for further directions hearings or an interim hearing. You can definitely find yourself in a 'rinse and repeat' situation at this stage of your matter.

Your trial

If you and your ex can't resolve your matter by negotiations or family dispute resolution, you will be given a date for a final hearing (the trial).

The trial date is typically about 18 to 36 months after the initiating application has been filed, but it can be even longer than that depending on the circumstances and complexity of your matter and the delays in the court.

At the trial, you and your witnesses (the people who have sworn affidavits on your behalf) must attend court to be examined under oath. At the trial, you and your lawyer will attend court, usually with a barrister who has been briefed about your matter (see chapter 12 for more on barristers).

After hearing the evidence, the judge will then make a decision to determine all of the matters before the court. Sometimes the judge will make a decision quickly. But on other occasions it can take a further six months to one year for a judge to deliver their judgment.

* * *

So, you can see there are undeniable benefits to settling your matter outside of court if you can. Court is a complicated, costly and time-consuming process.

WHAT PARENTING ORDERS CAN THE COURT MAKE?

This book is focused on how to help your children get through your separation, so this section will only cover information about orders that are relevant to your kids. The property stuff I will save for a future book.

A parenting order is a set of orders made by a judge about parenting arrangements for your kids. The judge can make a parenting order based on an agreement reached between you and your ex. These are called 'consent orders'. Or the judge can make orders after an interim hearing or a trial.

When a parenting order is made, any person affected by the order must follow it. Parenting orders can deal with the following:

- who the kids will live with
- how much time the kids will spend with you and their other parent, and with other people such as grandparents
- the allocation of parental responsibility
- how the kids will communicate with you and your ex when they are not with you
- any other aspect of the care, welfare or development of your kids.

It's really important that you get some independent legal advice in relation to your situation. A family lawyer can help you understand your legal rights and responsibilities. They can also explain how the law applies to your unique situation.

The Family Relationship Advice Line can help you with free legal advice and information about services that can assist you. You can call them on 1800 050 321.

I've included in appendix A some other kinds of issues that can be the basis of a parenting matter filed with the court. The information has been adapted from the Family Court of Australia website, which is an excellent resource that you should explore if you are considering going to court.

OTHER OPTIONS BESIDES GOING TO COURT THAT ARE WORTH CONSIDERING

I don't know about you, but I'm exhausted just thinking about the court process. And I'm a lawyer who gets involved in the court process on a regular basis.

I encourage you to think about the future and, if possible, to work with your ex to solve common problems. Now I get that this may not always be possible, and it depends very much on your unique circumstances. But giving yourself the chance to try a more amicable way to get your future parenting plans on track will give you a better path forward.

I explain to my clients that there are six different pathways you can take to finalise your matter – but don't be daunted by that. Having a choice allows you to take control of your future.

The pathway you choose depends on your unique situation and the relationship you have with your ex. For example, if you are able to communicate well with each other and you plan to stay friends after the split, you might consider reaching an agreement that is amicable, collaborative, and takes into account the needs and wishes of both of you. Alternatively, if you find yourself not being able to be in the same room as your ex, and you hold no faith in negotiating with them, there may be ways to move forward without having to go directly down the court route.

Here's my 'Family Law Dispute Resolution Menu'. Similar menus are commonly used by competent family lawyers all over Australia. It's no secret that there is a large number of us who really truly do not want to see your family ending up in court.

Your family law dispute resolution menu

Kitchen table	Negotiation	Mediation	Collaborative practice	Arbitration	Litigation
? % success	40% success	65% success	85–90% success	Awards given	Are there ever any winners?
Quick if you both agree	Depends on how amicable you are	1 week–3+ months	3–6+ months	2–4 months	1.5–3+ years
• Entirely driven by you and your partner, figuring it out yourselves. • May be a power imblance.	• Driven by you both and can be assisted by lawyer. • Win/win as long as there is no power imbalance. • Can be some pressure to reach agreement even if not in your best interest.	• Driven by you both or professionally driven. • Potential pressure to resolve matter. • Can create win/lose outcomes. • May be under the threat of litigation.	• Driven by you and your former partner. Interest-based. • A series of 4–5 way meetings. • Open sharing of information. • No threat of litigation. Involvement of other non-legal professionals. • Win/win outcomes.	• You and your former partner control the process. • Shorter timeframe than court. • Private. • Can be used to resolve all or part of a dispute.	• Lawyer/court driven. • Win/lose. • High fees. • Creates division. • Emotional toll. • Lengthy timeframe. • Negative impact on ongoing relationships.
$ minimal cost	$$ $500–$3k+	$$ $2k–10k+ (subject to whether legally assisted)	$$$ $10k–$30k+ (subject to the issues, meetings and professionals)	$$$ $10k–$50k+ (subject to the issues)	$$$$$ Endless

Let's look more closely at some of these options which can help you reach agreement and keep you out of court.

Mediation

This pathway can help you to resolve your dispute with the help of a neutral person: a mediator. The goal of mediation is to of course reach an agreement with your ex that can be turned into either a parenting plan or consent orders.

Mediators are not there to make judgments or to take sides. You should think of a mediator as the 'chair' of a meeting between you and your ex. Their role is to facilitate proactive discussions in a safe, controlled environment that gets you to a resolution that is in your kids' best interests.

There are several options for finding a suitable mediator. The most cost-effective way is to use the Family Relationship Centres, Relationships Australia or other public and community-based services. You can also organise a private mediator, but this can cost more. However, the benefit of a private mediator is often that you can start your mediation sooner as the public and community-based services do tend to have long wait lists. Another benefit of using a private mediator is that you can research and find a mediator with the particular skills or personality that are a good fit for you and your ex to work with. Your family lawyer can help you find someone suitable, and can discuss with you whether they should come along with you to support you through the process. It can be helpful to have your lawyer with you, to get advice on the spot about your legal rights and the impact of any proposal.

Mediation is probably not suitable if you have experienced family violence in your relationship.

From my experience, the key to success with mediation is to be prepared. It's also helpful if you can approach it with an open mind, ready to listen and to work towards an amicable resolution.

If no agreement can be reached in mediation, the mediator will issue you with an 's60I certificate'. With this certificate, you can start proceedings in court if need be.

Collaborative practice

Collaborative practice requires you both to enter into an agreement to not initiate or threaten court proceedings. You both agree to negotiate openly, honestly and respectfully, and to work together to find solutions. Sounds good, doesn't it?

Collaborative practice may work if you are seeking an out-of-court settlement. It will suit you if you think that you and your co-parent are willing to negotiate in good faith, sharing information and considering input and advice from your lawyers and other professionals (like a child expert, for example) to create constructive future arrangements for your family.

On the flipside, this pathway may not be right if you or your co-parent think that the process will allow either of you to give less than full and frank disclosure. It also may not be suitable if there is a history of family violence, or where either of you wish to 'have your day in court'.

Arbitration

Property matters can be arbitrated, but it is not possible to arbitrate parenting matters. However, if your situation includes both parenting and property issues, it can really help to resolve the property part of your matter through arbitration, so you can concentrate on then reaching agreement about your kids.

Because this book is all about your kids, I'm not going to spend too much time on arbitration. But for your information, it's a process where you and your ex-partner, through your lawyers, present arguments and evidence to an Arbitrator. The Arbitrator then makes a determination to resolve the dispute and issues their decision (the 'award') within 28 days. This is so much quicker than the court process.

Arbitration is voluntary, and can be undertaken by agreement between you and your ex or by direct court referral. And when a decision is made by the Arbitrator, it's registered with the court and has the effect of a court order.

HOW LONG DOES COURT TAKE?

If you're heading for court, be sure to pack your sturdy shoes, plenty to read and lots of sandwiches. Oh, and make sure you also pack your steely resolve and every bit of strength you can muster. Am I making this sound like a Tolkien-esque kind of journey? Damn right I am!

I don't mean to scare you ... not really, anyway. But I am going to repeat what I've already mentioned in this book:

> IT IS NOT UNCOMMON FOR FEUDING PARENTS INVOLVED IN FAMILY LAW PROCEEDINGS TO HAVE TO WAIT UP TO THREE YEARS AFTER FILING FOR THEIR ISSUES TO BE RESOLVED.

Just think about that for a minute.

If your kid is eight when court starts for your family, they could very well be close to being a teenager by the time a judge makes a decision. That's a serious amount of time and money, taken away from you and your kids, in what should be a wonderful time in all of your lives – getting your family on track after separation and living your best lives.

Courts take a seriously long time to resolve disputes. Think very carefully before you head out on the journey. Take some time upfront to properly explore all your other options.

* * *

It is my greatest wish that you and your co-parent can work together to figure out the best way to manage the care of your children. But, I get it can sometimes be the case that you have no other option but to commence court proceedings. Or, perhaps your ex has forced your hand and you find yourself in the court system. If this is you, the best thing you can do is keep the best interests of your children in mind, always. This will greatly assist in ensuring that your kids get through the splits as positively as possible.

Chapter 10

WHY YOUR KIDS' WISHES ARE IMPORTANT IN COURT

'Your kids may not say the same things to you and your ex, and you may only be hearing what you want to hear.'

WANTING TO HAVE A SAY

It will come as no surprise that once you have separated, your kids are likely to want to take part in determining what their future looks like. This is even more so as children get older and start to develop the maturity and foresight to know their own happiness is key to them thriving.

The way kids can have their say comes in many shapes and forms.

From my experience in working with separating families, and especially in my role as an Independent Children's Lawyer, there are two groups of kids. The first group wish they could rewind to a time when you were together with your ex. In fact, even if things start to get a little better after the split, and you might be communicating like an ace with your ex, many kids start to want their parents together again. It's normal for children to wish for their parents to get back together, and it's a wish that possibly will not go away for a very long time.

The second group of kids are those little cherubs who try to fix things. I call them the 'Fix It Kids'. Fix It Kids spend lots of time and imagination trying to find ways to fix things to either get their parents back together or smooth the way for more civil conversations between parents.

Fix It Kids try lots of things to repair your relationship. They promise to behave better and to be the 'perfect' kid, so that you will stop arguing with your ex. Some Fix It Kids will act out or misbehave, so that you might put aside your issues and focus on them instead.

Other Fix It Kids might tell you that they feel sick with stomach aches, headaches or anxiety, so you will come together with your ex to care for them. I am of course not suggesting that your kids are lying to you when they tell you they are sick, but it can be helpful to keep an eye out for those phantom moments when a headache might not actually be a headache.

During my time practising in family law, I have also seen Fix It Kids doing their best to create reasons for their parents to see each other. For example, kids might deliberately leave items they need at their dad's house or ask Mum if Dad can visit.

If trying to fix the relationship doesn't work, sometimes they will try to manage the separation process. You might be experiencing your kids taking on an adult role, like doing their best to keep the peace, giving you suggestions about what to say to your ex at the next meeting, or even working out complicated logistics for you.

It's a good idea to remind them that their job is to be a kid and that your job is to be the parent. It's also helpful to remember your kids are not there to support you. That's a job for other adults in your life such as a trusted friend or family member, or a professional support person.

Your kids need to hear you speaking about a positive future. Part of that positive outlook can include saying to your children that wishing and hoping are a normal part of divorce. When things happen that we aren't happy about, we of course hope those things will change.

It's vital for kids to know they don't cause a separation. And kids can't fix a divorce, no matter how much they wish they could. Tell your kids that even though you can't change things, it's important for them to talk about how they feel. Tell them that talking about their feelings will help you to know how they feel, and when you know how they feel you can try to make things better for them.

GIVING YOUR KIDS A VOICE

Give your kids a voice and let them know they can be open about their wishes.

> In around 2018, I met a wonderful dad whose wife had left him and moved overseas. The wife left their 10-year-old daughter with the dad and started her new life in China. The dad had a wonderful support structure around him, with a helpful sister and an elderly but spritely mother, who became known to me as 'the girls' because that is how the dad affectionately referred to them.
>
> The dad came to see me to get some advice about how he should move forward legally with the care of his daughter. However, as we talked about his situation, it became clear that his main concern was about how the wife's disappearance would impact his daughter, and whether his daughter wanted to try to foster her relationship with her mother.
>
> The dad just wasn't sure what his daughter wanted. He didn't know whether she wanted to continue a relationship with her mother, which he was ready to support, or whether she needed time to adjust to a new life, possibly without her mother involved.
>
> The dad and 'the girls' came up with a great idea to help the daughter start to think about what she wanted to do and say. They decorated the outside of a shoebox with the daughter and made a 'Wishes' label for the box. Each time the daughter had a thought or a wish about her mother, she was encouraged

to put into the box a small piece of paper with the thought or wish written on it. The dad also wrote a description that read something like this:

> *I am a wishing box and I can hold your wishes. Some of your wishes will come true and some will not. Don't forget that all of your wishes are very real and are very important. You can add new wishes whenever you like or you can take away old ones.*

The wishing box helped him to have conversations with his daughter about whether she wanted to try to contact her mother in China.

It's important to give your kids the opportunity to speak their truth, whatever that is at the time. But it's also important to accept that kids change their minds, and they should be encouraged to feel safe in being honest about their wishes for the future.

However it's also important to remember that although kids may have strong desires about, for example, who they want to live with, this is only one consideration that the court takes into account when determining arrangements.

WHAT THE COURT DOES ABOUT YOUR KIDS' WISHES

It's common for parents to have the view that their kids should be able to decide where and with whom they live, and how much time they spend with each parent. This can especially be the case with parents of teenagers, who struggle to figure out how they will get their strong-willed young humans to do what is necessary, rather than whatever they want.

I can't tell you how many times I've had clients say to me, 'he wants to live with me', or, 'she doesn't want to see Mum/Dad.' I want to drop a truth bomb right now: your kids may not say the same things to you and your ex. You may only be hearing what you want to hear, or the child may be telling you that just to make you happy. It is for this reason the court not only takes the views of your kids into account, but a list of other considerations also comes into play (see further below).

There are several ways the court considers the wishes of the kids and gathers evidence about what is in your kids' best interests. The court can use a range of alternatives either separately or combined to work out what the wishes of the children are. These include:

- a Child Dispute Conference, where the court receives evidence and a summary of issues, prepared by a qualified Family Consultant
- Family Reports prepared by a Family Consultant, who is usually a psychologist
- evidence from other expert witnesses – the court can sometimes receive evidence from a psychologist or psychiatrist about the kids
- the appointment of an Independent Children's Lawyer to represent the kids and put their views before the court.

These different roles are discussed in more detail in later chapters.

It's important to understand that your children cannot be forced to express their wishes. If they do not want to say what their view is they do not have to. The court is focused on not placing undue stress on kids. It is vitally important that kids do not feel the weight of the decision about where they live is on their shoulders.

Do kids give evidence?

The *Family Law Act* doesn't prohibit kids from giving evidence but permission must be granted by the court before a kid can be called as a witness. It is an extremely rare occurrence, and I have personally not come across this situation in my experience as a family lawyer.

Additional considerations

The additional considerations the court must look at in determining parenting orders are:

1. Any views expressed by the children, taking into consideration the children's age and level of maturity.

2. The nature of the relationship of the children with each parent and other significant people including grandparents.
3. The willingness and ability of each of the children's parents to facilitate and encourage a close and continuing relationship between the children and the other parent.
4. The likely effect on the children of any changes to the children's circumstances including the effect on the children of any separation from one of their parents or another child or person who is significant.
5. The practical difficulty and expense of children spending time with the other parent.
6. The capacity of each of the children's parents to provide for the needs of the children, including emotional and intellectual needs.
7. The attitude to the children and to the responsibilities of parenthood demonstrated by each of the children's parents.
8. Any family violence to which the children have been or might have been directly or indirectly exposed.

Whether or not a parent has fulfilled their duties depends on the extent to which each of the parents has:

1. participated in making decisions about long-term issues in relation to the children
2. spent time with the children
3. communicated with the children
4. facilitated, or failed to facilitate the other parent:
    a) participating in decisions about the children;
    b) spending time with the children;
    c) communicating with the children; and
4. fulfilled or failed to fulfil their obligations as a parent to maintain the children.

* * *

Remember, it is natural and necessary that once you have separated, your kids will want to take some part in determining what their future looks like. This is even more important as kids get older. It can be difficult to accept, but keep in mind that sometimes, kids might be telling you how they want their future to look, and at the same time communicating a completely different idea to their other parent. Let your kids have a voice and listen to them. Be guided by their wishes, but also by the professional advice you receive throughout your separation journey.

Chapter 11

THE LAWYER

'I think most people who find themselves in a separation situation just want to get their matter finalised and move on with their lives.'

I have included this part of the book to give you information about the types of professionals who may get involved in your family law matter, depending on what pathway you choose to take to reach a settlement with your ex. Giving your kids some details about who a lawyer is, or a barrister or a judge, can go a long way towards assisting them in understanding the court process and, importantly, realising these professionals are all humans who have a job to do.

As you would know by now, I'm a family lawyer. I've been doing this gig for many years and, wow, have I met lots of different kinds of lawyers.

There are lawyers who love a fight, lawyers who are too busy to get to your matter, and lawyers who don't have experience in family law but think it can't be that hard to figure it out.

On the flipside, there are also kind lawyers, lawyers who focus on alternative ways of reaching a settlement without going to court, collaborative lawyers and lawyers who are completely vested in your matter.

I try to be one of the kind lawyers. I'm a collaborative family lawyer and I work hard to help my clients take as peaceful a path as possible. But sometimes, especially when it comes to figuring out the best interests of kids, it can be difficult to keep things peaceful. This is especially so if you are in a situation where your ex is difficult or there has been a history of family violence, or even if you each see the needs of your kids very differently.

Most importantly, I think most people who find themselves in a separation situation just want to get their matter finalised and move on with their lives. But, if there are issues that cannot be easily resolved, your family lawyer should always be ready to stand up for you and do what is necessary to ensure you get an outcome that is as close as possible to ensuring the best interests of your kids are met.

WHAT DOES YOUR LAWYER DO FOR YOU?

You've probably heard your friends or family speak about 'my lawyer' or 'my solicitor' when they tell you about their family law problems. But what does a family lawyer actually do?

Your family lawyer is responsible for dealing with legal issues that come up between you and your ex. Your lawyer represents you in court if need be, and is skilled in being able to negotiate on your behalf.

If you've separated from your partner or are thinking about separating, it's always a good idea to obtain some preliminary advice from an experienced family lawyer. You can ask your lawyer for advice about:

- the breakdown of your relationship
- parenting arrangements
- property settlement rights and obligations
- whether or not child support is payable to you or by you
- filing a divorce application or helping you manage your own divorce.

A family lawyer is a solicitor who is particularly interested and skilled in family law work. Sometimes they can also assist you in other areas, such as preparing a Will, acting on your behalf in the sale of a family home, or payment of settlement money to your ex. But not all family lawyers do this other work as it's common for family lawyers to be highly specialised and focused solely on their area of law.

If you do need advice on other areas of law, your family lawyer should be well placed to match you up with another suitably qualified lawyer.

A good family lawyer is experienced in dealing with family law issues on a daily basis. They live and breathe family law. They can give you advice that is specific to your unique circumstances, negotiate a settlement for you, represent you in court or at mediation if needed, and ensure your interests – and your children's – are protected.

HOW ARE YOU INVOLVED?

Your involvement with the family law process can be as much or as little as you feel comfortable with or need. But at the very least, you need to be able to tell your lawyer what you would like to do. This is referred to as giving your lawyer your 'instructions'.

The more involved you are in your matter, the more you can save on costs and the more you will understand about your legal situation. Ways that you can get more involved include:

- Get any relevant documents together and send them to your lawyer. In parenting matters this can include any relevant emails and/or text messages between you and your ex, school reports, medical reports and counselling notes.
- Stay in regular communication with your family lawyer and insist on frequent updates.
- Be available to speak with or meet with your family lawyer when they ask you to. Make your relationship with your family lawyer a priority.

- Carefully read any written advice from your family lawyer, and if you don't understand something, ask for clarification or organise a meeting so you can ask questions.
- Carefully read any letters or emails from your ex's lawyer (or from your ex if they are self-represented). It's important you stay on top of this so you are on the same page as your family lawyer.
- Help your family lawyer by keeping a regular chronology of events during the separation.
- Be open to all options that your family lawyer puts to you, and really take the time to consider advice.

HOW TO CHOOSE THE RIGHT FAMILY LAWYER FOR YOU

Okay, so you've worked out that you need a family lawyer. Now what? How are you going to choose the right lawyer?

This can be daunting because it's possible you have never had to get a lawyer before. Plus, you are probably in a situation where you are having to make important decisions on your own, while your emotions are all over the place and you have lots of issues to deal with. Add into the mix that there are lots and lots of boutique family law firms to choose from and it can be tricky to know where to start.

I've put together a checklist of 10 things you should consider doing to make sure you choose the right family lawyer for you:

1. Choose a specialist family lawyer.
2. If you can, get a referral from someone you trust.
3. Align your values.
4. Understand that it's okay for your family lawyer to be a 'straight talker'.
5. Avoid the lawyer who promises you the world.
6. Interview your potential family lawyer before you commit to them.
7. Make sure you are getting independent legal advice.

8. Go with your gut.
9. Ask about legal fees and ask for a realistic quote.
10. Empower yourself.

Let's look at each of these.

1. Choose a specialist family lawyer

There are lots of lawyers around but they don't all practise in the family law space. Or, they may dabble in family law but they also have their fingers in lots of other pies. I suggest you look for a lawyer who practises exclusively in family law.

Family law is a large and complex area that is always evolving. It takes an expert in family law to support you effectively on your family law journey.

2. Get a referral from someone you trust

I reckon that referrals are the best way to make decisions on who to go with in all service areas. If you're lucky enough to have a recommendation from a family member or a friend you trust, it can make your journey to finding your family lawyer so much easier.

If you can't get a referral from someone you know and trust, try Google, and take some time to review a potential family lawyer's website. You should be able to get a vibe of their values and the way they operate. You can also reach out to single parent groups or other Facebook groups to see if anyone is happy to share their experience with their family lawyer.

3. Align your values

Family lawyers have different styles of lawyering. Some are litigious, which means they like to put on the gloves and get into a courtroom as quickly as possible. You'll know these lawyers when they say to you in an initial meeting, 'Let's just file', without talking to you about your other options.

Other family lawyers take a more collaborative approach, where they are focused on resolving your matter without going to court.

Have a think about your values, and work out whether your potential family lawyer has the same values as you.

4. It's okay for your family lawyer to be a 'straight talker'

Sometimes the advice I give to potential clients in our initial meeting may not be what they want to hear.

But guess what? That's the job of a lawyer – to give you proper advice about your situation. Your lawyer shouldn't get all Willy Wonka on you and sugar-coat stuff. Your lawyer's job is to tell you about the risks, and to work with you to come up with strategies and give advice on how to prevent potential negative outcomes for you and your family.

If you don't like what you hear at first, remember that the lawyer isn't there to win you over with comments like, 'we can win this,' or, 'you'll get a great outcome with me'. In fact, if you are hearing phrases like this, tread carefully, which brings me to my next point ...

5. Avoid the lawyer who promises you the world

As a family lawyer, I am not an oracle. I do not have a crystal ball to tell you what outcome you will receive or what a judge will order in your matter.

Be wary of the lawyer who makes big promises to you.

There are so many variables in family law matters, and so much depends upon your unique situation and the situation of your ex. Your family lawyer needs time to unpack that information. Getting 'slam dunk' advice in your first meeting can be premature. Watch out for this.

6. Interview your potential family lawyer before you commit to them

Yep, I mean it. Get along to an initial consultation or at least have a conversation over the phone or by video conference and meet the lawyer. This should give you a good idea of the type of family lawyer you would like to work with. Be prepared with your list of questions prior to each interview, and take your time to get to know them.

If it doesn't feel right, it's okay to leave it there, thank the lawyer for their time, and move on. Just because you speak with a family lawyer over the phone or pay to sit with them for an hour and a half at an initial meeting does not mean you are obliged to move forward with them.

7. Make sure you are getting independent legal advice

You should choose your family lawyer independently of your ex. It is not up to your ex to guide you to a lawyer. It is not up to your ex to tell you that you do not need a lawyer. If this is happening to you, it can be disempowering and is in fact a form of coercive control, which is family violence.

8. Go with your gut

No matter how many years a family lawyer has been practising, no matter what specialist accreditations, further studies or awards are hanging up in their office, if you don't feel good vibes then they are not for you.

Trust your gut reaction – this is the person you will be speaking to about your deepest fears and concerns, the care of your kids, and your future dreams and aspirations. Don't do that with someone who doesn't make you feel confident and at ease.

9. Ask about legal fees

Law firms have different ways of charging. Some offer fixed-fee services while others offer traditional billing per hour. There are pros and cons to both options, but my preference is a fixed-fee model.

In my experience, engaging a family lawyer can strike fear into the best of us, mainly because of the fees. Those law firms that invest in online solutions to make sure their running costs are lower can work well in a fixed-fee model. Personally, I don't think it's right to charge $45 for a five-minute phone call. In a fixed-fee arrangement, your phone calls and emails are all part of the agreement, which gives you and your family lawyer the time to develop a genuine relationship.

A fixed-fee arrangement helps you know what your costs will be. You will know when you must pay and how much you need to manage your account. And importantly, your family lawyer is encouraged to be more efficient to achieve results.

If you can't afford a family lawyer, you should reach out to your local Legal Aid office to find out if you are eligible for a grant of Legal Aid. This means that the government will assist you by providing you with a suitably qualified family lawyer, at no cost to you. There are strict guidelines for whether you are eligible for this support. Check out the Legal Aid Means Test Indicator if you think you could be eligible. Legal Aid also look at the merit of your matter, which means they look at whether you are likely to succeed in your case and whether providing aid to you will achieve what you want. There is a different means test and merit test for each state and territory and you should contact your local Legal Aid office or check out each state's or territory's website for more details.

10. Empower yourself

Most of the time, the family law process will be new to you, and like anything new that you have to undertake in times of stress, it can be intimidating.

Choosing a family lawyer who is right for you should put you at ease by helping you to understand what to expect and what steps you can take to get your matter finished. If you leave an initial meeting with your potential family lawyer and you feel like you've been heard, you've been informed, you have clarity and you feel empowered, that's a good sign.

WHAT ABOUT REPRESENTING YOURSELF?

Sometimes a person will need to represent themselves if they can't afford a lawyer and can't access Legal Aid. Or, a person might try to reach agreement with their ex, especially if they are amicable, without the help of a family lawyer.

My view is that if you find yourself on the pathway to court, you should at the very least get some initial advice from a family lawyer. But, if you have separated and are amicable with your ex, you might find you can reach an agreement without the help of a lawyer. There may be no need to rush off and get advice. Take your time and see how far you can get between you.

If you can reach agreement with your ex without the help of a lawyer then I take my hat off to you and support you wholeheartedly. You should still come to a family lawyer with your agreement clearly written out, so you can get advice on whether the agreement should be formalised in consent orders or another kind of agreement.

Some people simply don't want to engage a lawyer at all. They may think that potential legal fees are too expensive in relation to the potential outcome, or they may consider themselves competent to run the matter themselves. It can't be that hard, right?

Here are some myth busts for you if you are thinking about self-representing.

Myth #1: Self-representing will save me money

Initially, you will save money. But, as your matter progresses, as a self-represented person, you should be aware that the court has the power to make orders for costs against people involved in litigation. The general rule in family law matters is that each person should bear their own costs. But if circumstances justify making a costs order against you, the court can do so. These circumstances can include:

- Poor conduct, including in relation to the orders you are seeking, whether you are properly disclosing information and how you go about inspecting documents.
- Whether you have been highly unsuccessful in your case.

So, being your own lawyer can in fact end up costing you a lot of money.

Myth #2: I can teach myself the law and figure it out as I go along

It's difficult even for the most capable self-represented person to get a proper understanding of the evidence that's relevant to court and the conduct required. The rules and legislation that govern the conduct of family law matters are complex. Self-represented people can, and often do, fall into the trap of filing false or misleading evidence, they fail to disclose material that should be available to the other parent, they waste the court's time by chasing ultimately unsuccessful issues, they waste the court's time by filing affidavits that contain lengthy or irrelevant material, and they make applications to the court that are either partly or wholly unsuccessful.

Myth #3: The family law jurisdiction is relatively simple to understand

The courts that hear family law cases are often referred to as 'Courts of impression'. That's because judges have a very wide discretion to make property orders that are just and equitable and parenting orders that are in the best interest of children.

Without a detailed understanding of how to present the facts of a case to the court, an understanding of whether an application is likely to succeed, or how to appropriately conduct yourself in a courtroom, it can be common for a self-represented person to achieve a poor outcome and be ordered to pay the costs of the other person.

* * *

Your family lawyer, if chosen well, will be your greatest ally. Be sure to find a lawyer whose values align with your own. And if your kids are interested, give them information about your family lawyer so they can have a clear picture about who your lawyer is and what they do. This can help to humanise the process for your kids.

Chapter 12

THE BARRISTER

'They are usually formidable, competent, confident and charismatic humans that I have the greatest respect for.'

Barristers conjure up all kinds of mental images, don't they? Serious-looking women and men in black flowing gowns and weird, old-fashioned white wigs. You can see them usually pulling a suitcase behind them or carrying thick folders in their arms. They are usually formidable, competent, confident and charismatic humans that I have the greatest respect for.

So, do you need a barrister for your family law matter? And if so, how much is that going to cost, and will you get to choose your own?

WHAT'S THE DIFFERENCE BETWEEN A LAWYER AND A BARRISTER?

Firstly, let's consider the difference between a lawyer and a barrister.

On a basic level, your family lawyer is a highly trained legal professional who focuses on your day-to-day legal matters. Your family lawyer can appear in court on your behalf, but they typically spend most of their time outside the courtroom.

A barrister is a lawyer who specialises in court advocacy, which means preparing arguments for hearings, as well as specialist legal opinions. They don't usually prepare court documents such as affidavits and orders, but they do advise on them. A barrister spends most of their time in court.

Whether you need a barrister depends on your situation. In my practice, I do recommend engaging a barrister if your case is heading to a final hearing. It's also a good idea to consider working with a barrister, alongside your family lawyer, if you need representation and advocacy with:

- specialised knowledge about family law
- detailed knowledge of the rules of evidence, and their application
- fully understanding litigation tactics
- the skills to identify the best case preparation
- the ability to persuade the other person, or the court, of the merits of your case.

Your family lawyer will no doubt have good working relationships with various barristers and will be able to identify the most suitable person to deal with your case, should the need arise.

The fees charged by barristers are generally proportionate with their experience and level of expertise. They can be grouped into four broad categories:

- **Reader:** after being admitted as a barrister, lawyers must 'read' for 12 months under a more senior barrister – referred to as a 'tutor'. There may be restrictions on the work a reader can do. Readers charge in the vicinity of $2,000 a day in family law matters.
- **Junior:** junior counsel are those barristers with around two to five years' experience. Juniors commonly charge between $2,500 and $4,000 a day.
- **Senior junior:** a senior junior barrister is counsel with more than five years' experience as a barrister. Rates for senior junior barristers start at about $4,000 a day.
- **Queen's Counsel and Senior Counsel:** Queen's Counsel (QC) and Senior Counsel (SC) are often referred to as 'silks'. This is because

their robes include a gown made of silk, whereas the gown of other barristers is made of cotton. Silks are those barristers who are recognised by the Bar Association as being outstanding advocates and legal advisors. In 1992, the Bar Association decided to change the name of all such new appointments to Senior Counsel from Queen's Counsel. There is no difference between QCs and SCs. Family law silks charge in the vicinity of $8,000 to $15,000 a day.

Some examples of where a more experienced barrister, as opposed to a junior barrister, may be crucial include:

- where the credibility of witnesses is central to determining the outcome of your case – in this kind of case, counsel accomplished in the art of cross-examination is crucial
- where your case involves complex legal issues such as trusts, equitable interests in property, relocations, Hague convention matters, and matters involving family and domestic violence
- where you need to present or challenge complex expert evidence
- where your case may be decided on the admission or rejection of particularly significant evidence.

Your family lawyer may suggest a barrister represent you for the following reasons:

- your family lawyer requires specialist assistance or a further opinion in relation to a complex issue in your case
- your family lawyer is unable to attend court on the day of your hearing
- your family lawyer feels that the case requires a specialist advocate or expert guidance
- you have a final hearing.

Many family lawyers are comfortable and well prepared to handle litigation, and it is usual for your family lawyer to run any smaller 'directions hearings', and even interim hearings.

Ordinary mums and dads can't afford a $12,000-a-day silk. But, if your case goes all the way to a final hearing, you will need a specialist advocate, a barrister, to represent you alongside your family lawyer.

WHY THE FANCY GARB?

Wigs made their first appearance in the 17th century in courtrooms purely and simply because that's what was being worn at the time. Wigs were essential wear for polite society.

Fast forward to the 21st century and barristers no longer wear wigs. They do however wear their 'robes'. Barristers are required to 'robe' for ceremonial sittings, judgments, trials, and contested hearings where oral evidence must be given. The robes include gowns, bar jackets and collars and tabs/jabots.

HOW TO CHOOSE THE RIGHT FAMILY BARRISTER FOR YOU

Ultimately the question of when and whether to hire a barrister is another variation of the question, 'How do I choose a good family lawyer?'

The best approach is to rely on personal references, professional reputation, publications and recommendations from your family lawyer. You should interview a barrister as you would any other professional: by asking many questions, and also relying on your gut.

ALWAYS KEEP AN EYE ON THE FEES

In 2017, there was a family law matter that was before Justice Benjamin. The case is known as *Simic & Norton* and it involved property and child custody. An Independent Children's Lawyer was also involved in the proceedings.

It's become a famous case because of Justice Benjamin's comments about legal fees.

You see, the case eventually settled on the seventh day of the final hearing. But by that time, the parents had outlaid an eye-watering

$860,000 in legal costs between them. Justice Benjamin described this as, 'outrageous levels of costs for ordinary people involved in family law proceedings'.

Justice Benjamin went on to say:

> In the Sydney Registry of the Family Court I have observed what seems to be a culture of bitter, adversarial and highly aggressive family law litigation. Whether this win at all costs, concede little or nothing, chase every rabbit down every hole and hang the consequences approach to family law litigation is a reflection of a Sydney-based culture by some or many litigants or whether it is an approach by some legal practitioners or a combination of both, I do not know.
>
> Which ever is the cause, the consequences of obscenely high legal costs are destructive of the emotional, social and financial wellbeing of the parties and their children. It must stop.'

I share this with you because I want you to take those rose-coloured glasses off and throw them away. Do your best to keep in the front of your mind the legal fees you are incurring. Reality check the path you are on regularly, and consider the options we have looked at earlier in this book to avoid ending up in court if you can. Whether it be with your family lawyer or a barrister, it's important you keep firm sight of what you are spending and whether there is another way to reach a settlement rather than spending hard-earned money to continue fighting in court.

* * *

If your kids are curious, you should take some time to explain the role of a barrister and perhaps show your kids some photographs of what a barrister wears and the job a barrister performs.

Chapter 13

THE INDEPENDENT CHILDREN'S LAWYER

'If you find that the ICL does not agree with your position, you should take some time to carefully consider what they say because, as an independent person, they have the ability to step back and look at the big picture.'

WHEN AND HOW DOES AN ICL GET INVOLVED?

If you find yourself in court – with either an application you have made or that you are responding to – about your kids, an Independent Children's Lawyer, or more commonly called an 'ICL', may be appointed by a judge to your matter.

The role of an ICL is not always understood by mums and dads, or by kids. The ICL's role to look at the 'best interests' of the children can be confusing because it may not be what you have experienced in the past (when you think about your own lawyer). It's basically a lawyer for your kids, not for you or your co-parent.

ICLs either work for Legal Aid or they are private family lawyers who have at least five years of experience in dealing with parenting matters in court. So, they're lawyers who know their stuff, and have also had specific training to become an ICL.

The appointment of an ICL to a case is funded by the government. This means that if the ICL appointed to your case is a private lawyer (a lawyer from a private firm as opposed to a Legal Aid lawyer), they are paid a significantly lower amount than they would normally earn to look after this kind of matter.

You may be asking, 'So what, Bron? Why do you raise this?'

Well, to be frank with you, an ICL can sometimes be run off their feet with other, more lucrative family law matters (the matters that pay their bills and their staff's salaries), and it can mean that their ICL work is not a priority. Now I'm not saying this would be the case in all situations. Working as an ICL is a very serious commitment, and I say this from personal experience. But if an ICL appointed to your matter is not getting back to you quickly, or their communication is a little unreliable, it is not from lack of care or responsibility for your matter but rather their other ongoing commitments. If you understand this, it may help if you are feeling frustrated about how your ICL is attending to your matter.

It helps to have patience with an ICL and grant them the respect they deserve in taking on such an important role for the court. It also will greatly assist you if you are kind and considerate towards an ICL appointed to your matter – as part of their discovery into the details of your matter they will look at your behaviour.

On the flipside to all this, if you have significant concerns about the ICL appointed to your matter, talk to your lawyer about it. They can then talk to the ICL on your behalf or raise concerns through the proper channels.

WHY DO MY KIDS NEED THEIR OWN LAWYER?

In family law proceedings, your kids won't usually attend court. An ICL acts as their voice, and is able to tell the court about your kids' welfare and views during the case.

In 2014, the Australian Institute of Family Studies recognised three main reasons for having an ICL involved in parenting proceedings:

- to facilitate the participation of the kids in the proceedings
- to gather evidence

- to be an 'honest broker' in managing the case and negotiating a settlement where possible.

Article 12 of the United Nations Convention on the Rights of the Child compels our courts in Australia to ensure the participation of kids in matters about their own care and to ensure their views are heard. This has been incorporated into our *Family Law Act*.

In her report titled, 'Laying the Guideposts for Participatory Practice: Children's participation in family law matters', Kylie Beckhouse (former Director of Family Law services at Legal Aid NSW and current Federal Circuit Court Judge) says that in parenting matters, the views and voices of our kids can be heard and considered in two ways:

- Kids can meet with an expert social scientist, who prepares a report that includes the views of the kids.
- Additionally, kids may have an ICL who is appointed to represent their best interests.

WHAT EXACTLY DOES AN ICL DO?

The role of the ICL is to present information to the court about your kids' welfare and views.

There are guidelines for ICLs to follow, that were endorsed in 2013 by the Chief Justice of the Family Court of Australia, the Family Court of Western Australia and also by the Federal Circuit Court of Australia. The guidelines include that the role of the ICL is as follows:

> The best interests of the child will ordinarily be served by the ICL enabling the child to be involved in decision-making about the proceedings. However, this does not mean that the child is the decision maker. Among the factors that indicate the appropriate degree of involvement in an individual case are:
>
> - The extent to which the child wishes to be involved; and
> - The extent that it is appropriate for the child having regard to the child's age, developmental level, cognitive abilities, emotional state and views.

These factors may change over the course of the ICL's appointment.

The ICL is to act impartially and in a manner which is unfettered by considerations other than the best interests of the child.

WHAT WILL HAPPEN IN THE FIRST MEETING BETWEEN THE ICL AND MY KIDS?

The ICL will want to work on having a warm and professional relationship with your kids. They will introduce themselves and allow a bit of time to get to know your children. They might ask your kids questions to start a conversation like:

- How was your day?
- If you weren't here, what would you normally be doing?
- What do you like to do after school?

The ICL will ensure your kids are comfortable and they will explain where you are (if you brought your kids to the meeting and you are, say, waiting in another room). The ICL will reassure your kids they will return to you after the meeting.

Your kids might be asked to draw a picture or asked about their personal interests.

The ICL will want to explain clearly what they would like to talk about in the first meeting, and will use words that are easily understood by your kids. The ICL might say something like, 'I'll tell you a bit about me and we'll also talk about why you're here. Then, if you want to, you can ask me some questions or tell me about your views. At the end, I'll check in with you about what we've talked about. Does that sound okay with you?'

In the initial meeting and beyond, the ICL will strive to give your kids clear and age-appropriate explanations about the legal process. They will explain to your kids that they are being heard (and not just listened to). They will have ongoing contact with them.

Try not to worry about how your kids will react to an explanation about the legal process. It's far better for your kids to get the explanation from a kind ICL than from your ex, where the information might be peppered with negative comments.

'Family Law: Working with Children – a good practice guide', prepared by Legal Aid New South Wales, clearly sets out the type of information an ICL will likely need to discuss or explain to your kids. According to the guide, there are 10 pieces of information that the ICL will likely cover with your kids. They include:

- Why your kids are there.
- Who the ICL is and what they do in the proceedings.
- That the ICL has been asked to help by the judge, and explaining what a judge is.
- That the ICL can tell the judge how the kids are feeling or what the kids are thinking about the proceedings, but that your kids do not have to say anything. It's important to remember that the key purpose of the meeting is to give the kids the opportunity to participate in the proceedings and express their views only if they wish to do so.
- When acting as a 'best interests' representative, that the ICL may also tell the judge what the ICL thinks is best for the kids, even if that isn't what the kids want.
- The limits of confidentiality, which means that the ICL can keep some things to him or herself, but not everything.
- When and if the ICL will see the kids again.

So the ICL can really help to talk about the kinds of procedural issues that kids commonly worry about, but may not be able to express, like:

- Will I have to go to court?
- Will the ICL tell my parents what I have said?
- Who is making the decisions?
- Do I have to see anyone else?

- When will all of this be over?
- What happens if my parents reach an agreement about me?

It's important that your kids can contact the ICL if they need to. The ICL will speak with your kids about how they can stay in contact. If your kids are too young to do this themselves, the ICL can set up other ways for the relationship to continue, like making contact with your kids' teachers so they can help.

WHEN DOES THE ICL MAKE RECOMMENDATIONS TO THE COURT?

Sometimes an ICL will be ready, early on in a matter, to know what orders they consider to be in the best interests of your kids. If this happens, they will tell your lawyer, or if you don't have a lawyer, they will tell you. This discussion can help with negotiations - especially if an ICL agrees with what you are proposing about orders for your kids. It can sometimes help your ex to understand your point of view if the ICL is agreeing with your position. (Remember, it's the lawyer for your kids, not for you.)

On the flipside, if you find that the ICL does not agree with your position, you should take some time to carefully consider what they say because, as an independent person, they can step back and look at the big picture. They might just be seeing something you have not. Try to keep your mind open to other points of view. And if you still feel your position is the right one, be respectful and take time to clearly set out why you have the position that you do.

In other cases, your kids' best interests may be unclear to the ICL and the ICL may not be able to make a recommendation until much later in your matter, or sometimes not at all.

It's important for you to know that an ICL can change their recommendation to the court. You see, the ICL's recommendation is based on the evidence available to them at the time. If new evidence comes into play before the court makes final orders, the ICL should consider the impact of this new evidence on their recommendations. An example of this would be if your ex was found to be taking drugs or drinking excessively when the kids were in their care. If there was new evidence about this, the ICL would probably review their recommendation if they had previously recommended the kids spend lots of time with your ex.

DOES THE COURT ALWAYS MAKE ORDERS THAT THE ICL RECOMMENDS?

No. The judge will listen to what everyone in the case says, including your and your ex's lawyers (or you if you are self-represented), as well as the ICL. The judge makes decisions based on all the evidence you and your ex are relying on.

WHAT ELSE CAN HAPPEN WHEN AN ICL IS APPOINTED?

The ICL is usually very helpful in encouraging and taking part in negotiations between you and your ex. They can play an important role in helping you to settle your matter in a way that is in your kids' best interests.

The ICL also continues to reality check the parenting arrangements as your matter progresses. They check to make sure that proper arrangements are made to protect your kids' interests, until your matter is finalised.

After your matter is finalised, whether you and your ex reach a settlement or the judge makes orders, depending on the age of your kids, the ICL may explain the court orders to them. The ICL is sometimes also involved for some time after your matter is finished in court, to follow up on arrangements about court orders.

THINGS YOU SHOULD REMEMBER IF AN ICL IS APPOINTED FOR YOUR KIDS

It's really important that your kids attend all appointments arranged by the ICL. Work with the ICL to make sure the appointments can fit in with your kids' schedules, and do your best to be flexible about this. If you can make it easy for the ICL to meet with your kids, the ICL will appreciate this.

The ICL is an independent representative for your kids. The ICL is not there to be a mouthpiece for them. Remember this if you find the ICL saying to you that they are limited in what they can discuss with you. It's important they remain independent, and discussing some things with you about the case may jeopardise their independence. The ICL is not going to become your new best friend or your confidante. They are trained not to do this and to remain impartial.

If you have a lawyer, anything you want to raise with the ICL should be raised by your lawyer, who will contact the ICL directly. If you are self-represented, it is likely the ICL will invite you to raise things with them in writing rather than having conversations over the phone or in person. This is to ensure the ICL remains impartial during your matter.

Chapter 14

THE OTHER PLAYERS

'The court is able to order you and your ex to attend an appointment with a Family Consultant and anything you say during the appointment can be written in a report.'

There are lots of ways that social scientists, counsellors, social workers, psychologists and psychiatrists might become involved in your family law matter.

Often, the practitioner can have a secondary role in providing your family with support or therapy. Sometimes, these practitioners are brought into your matter to prepare a family report, give evidence as a therapist to you or your kids, or are named in orders to provide therapy.

If you are in court about your kids, you may have already heard the following terms:

- Family Consultant
- Family Report
- Single Expert Witness
- Family Counselling
- Private Family Report Writer.

There can be some confusion about how these roles and responsibilities differ – this chapter aims to clear that up for you.

THE ROLE OF A FAMILY CONSULTANT

A Family Consultant is a qualified social worker or psychologist, with the skills and experience to work with kids and their families.

A Family Consultant appointed under regulation 7 of the Family Law Regulations 1984 is appointed by the court and is part of the court's personnel. These practitioners are sometimes referred to as 'Reg 7' consultants. They must be registered as a psychologist or be members of the Australian Association of Social Workers. They must also have a minimum of five years of post-graduate relevant experience.

The role of the Family Consultant is to help you and your ex, and the court, in your family law matter. They do this by providing advice, reports and recommendations from a social science perspective about the best interests of your kids. They are often appointed by the court to help parents and judges achieve the best possible outcome for children. Family Consultants are experts in kids' matters.

The court can request a Family Consultant to prepare a report to outline the issues in your case. The court can order you and your ex to attend an appointment with a Family Consultant, and anything you say during the appointment can be written in a report. That report then becomes evidence in your matter and the judge reads it.

Some of the specific things a Family Consultant does are:

- assisting and advising parents involved in family law proceedings
- assisting and advising the court, including giving evidence at final hearings
- helping parents resolve their disputes
- preparing a report
- advising the court about appropriate future support for your family, such as whether you should meet with a Family Counsellor or dispute resolution practitioner, and recommending courses or programs you and/or your ex can do.

What exactly is a Family Report?

In difficult parenting cases, the court will order a report to be written about the kids, their parents and anyone else involved in the matter.

If an ICL has been appointed to your matter, it is usually this person who asks the judge to make an order for a Family Report to be prepared. Your lawyer can ask for this as well.

The Family Report is prepared by a Family Consultant, social worker, child and family psychologist or psychiatrist, depending on the issues in the case. The information for the report is gathered by interviewing your kids, you, your ex and any other people involved with the children. If you have a new partner, they can also be interviewed.

The Family Report can sometimes assist you in negotiating with your ex to settle the case. If your case is not settled, the report will become evidence that the judge will consider when making final parenting orders.

When preparing the Family Report, the Family Consultant considers your family's circumstances, explores issues relevant to your case, and recommends arrangements that will best meet your kids' future care, welfare and developmental needs. The best interests of your kids are the main focus of this report.

The report is formally released to the court before you or your ex receive it. The report cannot be shown to anyone except you and your ex and your lawyers. You can't show the report to other people, including your kids, their grandparents, your best friend, or your mate down at the pub, unless the court gives you permission. Even people who have been interviewed for the report, such as your new partner, cannot be shown the report without the court's permission.

What happens at the interviews?

The Family Consultant will run a series of interviews in one day or perhaps over a few days, depending on your availability. They will have an individual interview with you and with your ex. They may also interview other significant people in your kids' lives, including brothers and/or sisters, step or half brothers and/or sisters, partners or grandparents.

Your kids will be seen separately from you or your ex. Your kids will be given an opportunity to express their views and wishes, but they are not expected to do so. The Family Consultant may also watch your children interacting with you, your ex and other significant people in separate observation sessions.

All information gathered by the Family Consultant is admissible in court. They are required to include all relevant information in their report, and they may also be asked to give verbal evidence at a final hearing.

Coaching your kids for family report interviews is not okay

Telling your kids what they should say during a Family Report interview is not a good idea.

The Family Report is a very important piece of evidence in your parenting case. Generally speaking, judges put significant weight on the recommendations made in a Family Report. And because of this, it can make or break your parenting application.

I think that because of this, some parents can be so concerned about how they and their kids come across to a Family Consultant that they tend to over-prepare. They can also make the mistake of telling their kids what to say to the report writer.

Family Report writers are experienced professionals, and they can generally tell when a kid has been coached because of the way the kid is relaying information to them.

If you coach your kids, the worst-case scenario is that the Family Report writer will pick up on this and discuss it in their report. The report writer may then raise serious concerns about your ability to encourage your kids' relationship with your ex, and this can impact their assessment of you.

What happens if you don't like what you read in the Family Report?

Remember that the Family Report is only one piece of evidence your judge will think about when making a final decision about your kids. The court is not bound by any recommendations made in the report, although the court will place significant weight on the report.

If you are not happy with the findings of the report, or there are facts that you believe have been incorrectly interpreted, you can ask your lawyer to raise those concerns with the Family Consultant or call the Family Consultant as a witness so they can be cross-examined in court at your final hearing.

BUT WAIT ... WHAT IS A SINGLE EXPERT WITNESS THEN?

A Single Expert Witness is appointed by agreement between parents or by the court to give evidence or to prepare a report on an issue. Their appointment and their role are covered in Chapter 15.5 of the Family Law Rules 2004 - so you may hear your lawyer or an ICL refer to a Single Expert Witness as a 'Chapter 15.5 Expert'.

A Single Expert Witness can be a private practitioner such as a social worker, psychologist or psychiatrist, who is asked to prepare a report at the joint request of parents or by order of the court. These reports are often referred to as 'family reports' but that is not actually correct.

The *Family Law Act* says that the opinion of a Single Expert Witness can be used as evidence, it must be agreed or demonstrated that they have specialist knowledge, their knowledge must be relevant to the issues, and their opinion must be based on facts seen by the expert. So, for example, if your kid suffers from ADHD and this will impact the best interests of your kid and how they should be cared for, you might consider trying to appoint a Single Expert Witness who has proven experience in ADHD.

WHAT'S THE DIFFERENCE BETWEEN A FAMILY REPORT, PRIVATE ASSESSMENT AND EXPERT REPORT?

In summary, the differences are as follows:

- **Family Report.** This is a report ordered by the court and prepared by a family consultant appointed by the court. There is no cost to you.
- **Private Report.** You can ask a private professional to undertake a family assessment and provide the court with a report. You have to pay for a private assessment.
- **Expert Report.** Sometimes, the court will require an expert to provide assessments, diagnosis and information which can't be provided by a Family Consultant. For example, the court may need a psychiatrist to provide a psychiatric assessment report for either you or your ex. An expert report is paid for by you and/or your ex.

WHERE DOES A FAMILY COUNSELLOR FIT IN?

A Family Counsellor can provide counselling services to you, your kids or your family as a whole, if you are impacted by family law proceedings.

The *Family Law Act* says that a Family Counsellor can help:

- parents who are dealing with personal or interpersonal issues in relation to marriage
- parents and children who are affected or are likely to be affected by separation or divorce, to deal with personal and interpersonal issues and issues about care.

Unlike a Family Consultant, a Family Counsellor cannot disclose what is said to them during a counselling session unless the disclosure is required or authorised by the court. Some reasons for disclosure would include where it's necessary to protect your children from a risk of harm or preventing or lessening a serious and imminent threat to life or the health of you or your kids.

* * *

There are lots of ways that social scientists, counsellors, social workers, psychologists and psychiatrists might become involved in your family law matter. Sometimes these practitioners can be brought in to prepare a Family Report, give evidence, or be asked or ordered to provide your family with therapy. It's helpful to understand the different roles of practitioners who can be involved, and if your kids are curious, explaining the different roles to them can help your kids feel like they are more in control of their future.

Chapter 15

THE JUDGE

'Know that they will have sleepless nights thinking about your matter in order to come to the best possible outcome for your kids.'

I really hope that you never have to meet a judge.

No ... really. I mean it. My greatest wish for you is that you never step foot into a courtroom, and you never have to look a judge in the eyes.

Now, don't get me wrong. Judges are wonderful people. They're clever, insightful, hardworking, sometimes kind, always considered and very well respected. Some of my greatest memories of being a family lawyer have involved my interactions with judges.

> I remember around five years ago, I appeared a little anxiously before Her Honour Judge Henderson (now the Honourable Justice Henderson). The courtroom was full of my legal colleagues and I was fronting up to run an interim hearing for a matter where I had only met my client two days earlier. My client was a lovely young mum who I'll call Jade. Jade was in court in response to the father's application to remove their son Henry from her care.
>
> The father had been extremely abusive towards Jade, and she continued to be a victim of technology abuse. The father was relentless in his online stalking of her, which was now a

police matter. He had also been physically abusive towards Henry to the extent that Henry had ended up in hospital with trauma to his head.

The issue before Her Honour at the interim hearing was whether Henry should spend overnight time with the father. I ran that interim hearing because Jade could not afford a barrister. I was pleased to be able do so, and I remember spending hours preparing for the showdown.

When I walked into the courtroom with Jade, just after 10am on the day of the interim hearing, I saw that the father had his family lawyer and a barrister present. That made me shake in my boots. It's never easy going up against a barrister.

We kicked off the interim hearing, and I recall turning to Jade and whispering to her, 'We've got this. Stay calm, and if it all gets too much, just close your eyes and count to 10.' I wanted to close my eyes and count to 10 myself, but alas, I was on my feet and making submissions to Her Honour.

Fast forward 40 minutes and Her Honour made her judgment. Henry was going to spend some supervised time with the father, but for now, no overnight time. Jade was happy and I was relieved. To my surprise, Her Honour then looked at me and said, 'Ms O'Loan, you have fought a valiant fight today. I understand you only came into this matter two days ago and I want to say to you that you have done a great service to your client and to the court. Thank you.'

My experience with judges has been similar throughout my career. I wonder if Her Honour really understood the positive impact her words would have on me. I wonder if she could see that I had been out of my comfort zone but that I sucked it up and got on with the job. They are wonderfully wise and insightful humans that I have the greatest respect for.

So, if you do find yourself on the pathway to court, don't be afraid of your judge or concerned about how they will work on your matter. They are, after all, humans. Know that you are in expert hands and your judge really cares about your situation. Know that they will have sleepless nights thinking about your matter in order to come to the best possible outcome for your kids.

THE ROLE OF A JUDGE

Judges are the most senior members of the court. They are appointed by the Governor-General, usually from the ranks of the legal profession.

If your matter isn't resolved at mediation, a judge will hear your case in a courtroom.

Judges conduct trials in a courtroom, where they make decisions (the orders) about parenting and/or financial matters.

In parenting matters, the judge's role is to determine the best interests of your kids. These determinations are generally made by considering a number of factors relating to your kids' circumstances and your and your ex's circumstances.

The judge can also ask for an Independent Children's Lawyer to be appointed for the kids and for a Family Consultant to assist.

HOW SHOULD I ADDRESS A JUDGE?

'Your Honour' is the proper way to address a judge in court. If you are writing to a judge, you should address them as 'Dear Judge'.

HOW SHOULD I ENTER A COURTROOM?

If you enter the courtroom when a judge or registrar (see below) is sitting, it is customary to bow your head as a sign of respect for the judicial process. If you are there to watch another case, sit quietly in the public gallery seating at the back of the court, and remember to turn your phone to silent.

If you enter the courtroom before the court is in session, the court officer will announce the judge's arrival by asking everyone in the room to stand. The court officer will then knock on the door three times, which is located up near where the judge sits. You should bow your head at the same time as the judge bows, and after the judge sits down you can also sit down.

When the judge leaves the courtroom, the court officer will ask you to stand, and again it is customary to bow your head when the judge bows. If you leave while the court remains in session, it is customary to stop at the door inside the courtroom, face the judge and bow your head before you quietly leave.

A BIRD'S EYE VIEW

Make no mistake. The judge has a bird's eye view of the courtroom, and can see and hear almost everything happening in the courtroom.

The judge sits at the front of the courtroom, at 'the bench', which is usually raised. They sit facing the rest of the courtroom and are able to pick up the smallest of movements and facial expressions from those that are facing the judge.

It is for this reason, if you find yourself in court, that you should try to keep your emotions in check, even though that can be very hard when you are feeling anxious, concerned, upset or even angry. Do your best to keep your facial expressions and body language in check because it can be distracting for the judge and can also be seen as disrespectful. If you have difficulty with this, a good tip is to sit on your hands and look down.

BUT I HAVE A REGISTRAR IN MY MATTER – WHAT IS THEIR ROLE?

A registrar is a court lawyer. If you are in court, you might have a registrar for your hearing. Registrars aim to prepare your case for trial if a decision by a judge is necessary – this gives you and your ex the opportunity to reach agreement without the need for a judge to become involved.

Senior registrars have powers that bring them closely in line with judges. Some of those powers are:

- to make a parenting order where the order is an order until further order, or made in an undefended case

- to make a recovery order
- to make a child maintenance order or urgent child maintenance order pending the completion of proceedings
- to order a passport or other travel document to be delivered to the court
- to make an order in relation to a parentage testing procedure, issue a declaration of parentage of a child or make an order requiring a person to give evidence in relation to the parentage of a child or in relation to a report of a parentage testing procedure
- to make certain orders to enforce compliance with orders under the *Family Law Act* affecting children, only if the order is made until further order, or if there has been consent between the parents
- to make a de facto or spousal maintenance order, an urgent maintenance order or to vary or discharge a maintenance order
- to make a property order or declaration in relation to property matters, where the order or declaration is until further order
- to make certain orders in relation to child support.

YOUR FAMILY LAWYER'S RELATIONSHIP WITH THE COURT

There are certain ways your lawyer must and should act when you are in court and when you are before a judge or a registrar. It's important you understand that your family lawyer has a duty to the court. That means that, in addition to our duties to you, we have other obligations under the law.

As an officer of the court, I must not only obey the law, but also ensure the efficient and proper administration of justice. As such, in dealing with the court, you will see your family lawyer doing the following:

- being diligent in following through on any undertakings, which is a promise to the court and is binding

- not misleading the court by telling them the wrong thing, or by not saying something important and relevant
- being frank in all responses and disclosures to the court
- being independent, which means to be free from personal bias
- acting with competence, honesty and courtesy towards the judge, other lawyers, your ex and witnesses.

* * *

If your kids are curious, it can be helpful to talk to them about the role of a judge. Remember to remind your kids that a judge is a human being and takes their responsibility to make decisions very seriously.

PART IV
A SAFETY CONVERSATION

'It's a big deal, it's hard to talk about, it happens behind closed doors, it's insidious – and it's past time to call it out.'

FAMILY VIOLENCE is sadly prevalent in our society. It includes a broad range of violent, threatening, coercive or controlling behaviours, most commonly used by men (but nevertheless also sometimes used by women) against their current or former partners.

Being exposed to or witnessing family violence can have a traumatic impact on kids. It is a form of child abuse that creates trauma, disrupts a kid's ability to form healthy attachments, and impedes their physical, emotional and mental development. Teenagers who witness or are exposed to family violence can develop complex needs related to mental health and behaviour management and can become depressed, anxious, have violent outbursts, start risk-taking behaviour and start to abuse substances.

It's a big deal, it's hard to talk about, it happens behind closed doors, it's insidious – and it's past time to call it out.

The purpose of including this part in the book is to ensure that the conversation about family violence is accessible to you. Whether you are a victim or know a victim, the following chapters have been written to give you some insight into how to continue the conversation about family violence and substance abuse, not just between yourself and your mates, but also with your children.

Chapter 16

DEALING WITH ADDICTION AND VIOLENCE

'They often know that it's going on, and even if they don't see it or hear it or experience it directly, they're still affected by it.'

Separation is a very difficult experience. This is especially so if you find yourself in a situation where you're trying to re-establish parenting roles with your ex. There can be communication difficulties, differing priorities, often different parenting styles, and perhaps even different lifestyles.

How can you move forward in your co-parenting relationship if your ex is struggling with substance abuse issues? How should you be managing your emotions, and at the same time encouraging your ex to get the help they need while making sure the safety and wellbeing of your kids comes first? And how can you ensure you and your kids stay safe if you are victims of family violence?

There's just not enough room in this book to properly cover these very important topics, but it would be remiss of me not to include some words to help you address your situation, especially if you find yourself nodding your head and saying, 'Yep, Bron, this is my story'.

HOW TO CO-PARENT WHEN YOUR EX IS ABUSING SUBSTANCES

Substance use and abuse is actually a spectrum. Substance use could be having a few drinks with friends on the weekend or with colleagues after work. But it could also be so much more than that.

You see, substance use can very quickly morph into abuse, and it's important that you are aware of the signs to look out for. Some of the general signs of use becoming abuse are:

- drinking more than intended in one sitting
- needing to increase the amount of a substance to get the same effect
- when the substance use starts to affect physical or emotional health, or a person's job or relationships
- when legal issues are involved.

When you have separated, you no doubt have less influence over what your ex does. But, you do have an impact on how their behaviour affects your kids:

- Being direct with your co-parent and having a conversation with them can help if you are concerned their substance use may be bordering on moderate to severe.
- A good place to start is to ask your co-parent how they are managing their stress, or their work/life balance. This may give you some information about any possible substance use as a stress management tool. And remember to stay focused on your children's safety and comfort as the priority and the primary topic of conversation.
- While it may be a difficult conversation to have, you might try suggesting that your co-parent see a professional to provide an accurate assessment of their substance use, if you are worried. There are numerous kinds of therapies for substance abuse, including support groups, one-on-one therapy, outpatient treatments and inpatient rehabilitation. There are plenty of

options available, and a professional can help guide your co-parent when they are ready.

- Importantly, if your ex has a substance abuse issue, you need to set healthy boundaries. It may seem counterintuitive, but you can have compassion and understand their situation and at the same time feel uncomfortable and unsafe exposing yourself or your kids to your ex.
- If you are concerned, you will need to set boundaries around when and how your kids spend time with your co-parent. You might organise a phone call or a Zoom call instead of face-to-face time, perhaps for some time after school or on Saturday mornings.
- If you already have a shared parenting arrangement and become aware that your co-parent has a substance abuse problem, it's important that you speak with your family lawyer when deciding how to reset your boundaries. It goes without saying that parenting time and any agreements or parenting orders should be reassessed if severe substance abuse becomes an issue. Your family lawyer can talk to you about the options you have for modifying arrangements if necessary.
- You might find yourself in a situation where your co-parent is having treatment or is in recovery for their substance abuse. It helps if you can educate yourself on how to support your co-parent, or at least co-exist in a helpful way. You might consider starting therapy yourself, going to meetings and support groups for family members of substance abusers, or tap into resources online to help you navigate through such a difficult time.
- On a positive note, co-parenting is possible with your ex who is in recovery. You can compassionately provide support by gathering more information and educating yourself, using direct communication, setting healthy boundaries, taking care of yourself and managing your kids' safety.

FAMILY AND DOMESTIC VIOLENCE AND THE SIGNS TO LOOK OUT FOR

I'm going to say right from the outset, family violence is *never* okay. We all know this. But it can be difficult calling family violence out.

A definition I came across when I was researching for this book is:

> Family violence is any threatening, coercive, dominating or abusive behaviour that occurs between people in a family, domestic or intimate relationship, or former intimate relationship, that causes the person experiencing the behaviour to feel fear.

My further reading reminded me that family violence is not an argument once in a while, it is a continuous pattern of abusive behaviour perpetrated by one person towards another, often using multiple tactics. Family violence is not just physical or sexual abuse. It can include many types of abuse, all of which are unhealthy and harmful.

It's important for you to be aware of the different types of family violence so that if you are experiencing these behaviours, you can call them out and get the support you need. I've included in appendix B a summary of the different types of family violence. If you feel you are experiencing or have experienced any of these situations, make contact with a counsellor or psychologist, or call 1800 RESPECT. Your family lawyer can also help point you in the right direction. Of course, if you ever feel in imminent danger, call the police immediately.

KEEPING YOURSELF AND YOUR KIDS SAFE FROM FAMILY VIOLENCE

Whether you are deciding to stay in your relationship or leave, you are the best judge of your own safety. But, no matter what you decide to do, you should think about your safety options, create a safety plan and put safety measures in place to help reduce the risk to you and your kids.

What can I do to minimise risk if I am staying?

Have a think about what you can do to keep you and your kids safe, especially when you sense that the violence may be escalating. Think about these six steps to minimise your risk:

1. Talk to neighbours you know and trust and ask them to call 000 if they hear violence or abuse coming from your home. You might also consider setting up a signal with your neighbours to alert them about your situation. An example would be you light a candle in the front window of your home if you feel unsafe, and this is a sign for your neighbours to contact the police.
2. Contact your close family and friends and set up a code word that you can text to them in case you need them to call 000 on your behalf. An example code word could be 'lamb', where you might text to your friend, 'wanna come over for a roast lamb dinner on the weekend?'
3. Plan and practise, with your children, your escape route from the home. Don't move to areas in the house where you can become trapped. Find areas that are free from weapons. Remember, the most dangerous spaces in a home are usually the bathroom, kitchen and garage.
4. Teach your children that their job is to stay safe, not to rescue you. Teach your kids how to call 000.
5. If your kids are old enough, practice a 'safe word' or a phrase with them. Let them know to get ready to leave the home if you say the safe words. An example could be 'ruby red', where you could say, 'it's ruby red time now'.
6. If you must leave the home, plan how you will do it. Know the location of your nearest police station or hospital and go there if you need to.

What should I do if I am planning to leave?

The time immediately after leaving a family violence situation can be very dangerous, but there are lots of things you can do to plan for your safety. When it comes time to leave the home, make a plausible excuse to leave, or leave while your abuser is not at home.

Plan these six steps so you are ready to go:

1. Only tell trusted people you are planning to leave and where you are planning to go. Think about whether you need to tell your kids, or if it would be safer for them to just go along with you without having to be burdened by the information.
2. Turn off location settings on your mobile phone and any other technology you are taking with you. Make sure you do this for your kids' devices too. If you suspect your abuser is accessing your technology, consider leaving these items behind.
3. Hide a bag with clothes, medication, keys and other important items that you can grab easily, or leave the bag with someone you trust.
4. Make copies or take photos of important documents such as your and your kids' passports, your driver licence, Medicare card, deed to your home, and any other important financial records. Consider leaving copies with a trusted friend or relative.
5. Prepare clothes for your kids, their medical records and medication, bottles and nappies, and some of their favourite toys.
6. If you have pets and they are leaving with you, take food and whatever equipment you need to travel, such as a lead, pet cage or a pet bed.

How can my kids and I stay safe after leaving?

The months after leaving a family violence situation are also very dangerous. You must be vigilant during this time.

Consider taking the following eight steps to ensure your and your kids' safety:

1. Think about getting an intervention order if you don't already have one. You can start this process by contacting your local police station.
2. Try to change your routine. This could mean leaving work or home at different times, doing your grocery shopping at a different place, or driving instead of catching public transport.
3. Let key people know about your situation. Update your boss or other colleagues and your kids' teachers. Have a discussion with them about what they should do if they are worried about your safety or the safety of your kids.
4. Research ways to make sure your home is secure, like changing the locks or installing an alarm, security lights and cameras.
5. Replace any technology your abuser set up for you, registered for you or had access to. This includes smartphones, iPads and other tablets, computers, smartwatches and TVs.
6. Block your abuser on Facebook, Instagram, Twitter, WhatsApp and any other forms of social media.
7. Change the passwords to all your online accounts, including social media, email, banking accounts, your MyGov login and your e-tag if you have one.
8. Redirect your mail and set up a post office box in a suburb that you are not living in.

HOW TO HELP YOUR KIDS MANAGE

Kids can have their own unique experiences of family violence. They can directly experience physical, sexual, psychological and financial abuse. They can experience threatening and coercive behaviour. And importantly, your children witnessing or being exposed to family violence directed at you is also family violence.

Family violence between parents is traumatic for kids. They often know it's going on, and even if they don't see it or hear it or experience it directly, they're still affected by it. Just knowing that your partner or ex-partner is hurting you is distressing and traumatic for your kids.

If you find yourself in an untenable situation, you should seek help with safety planning and to explore your options. For your kids, the Kids Helpline is a wonderful resource. Their contact number is 1800 55 1800 and they provide free, confidential 24/7 phone and online counselling for people aged 5 to 25 years.

Talking about the situation

Family violence is a difficult topic to talk about with your kids. But chances are that if they are experiencing family violence (and remember, that can be if they are witnessing you being abused), they will want to - and should - talk about it with someone.

Do your kids a favour and make sure they have access to a counsellor or a psychologist. At the very least, ensure your kids have a close and trusted extended family member, mentor or friend they can talk to.

Here are some general statements you can use when talking to your kids about family violence:

- Family violence is not your fault, even if your parents are fighting about you or you didn't clean your room or did something wrong.
- Family violence is not okay - grown ups have lots of ways to solve their problems. Violence or abuse should never be one of them.
- You have a right to be safe: don't get in the middle of a fight. The best thing to do is call someone to help.
- Your feelings are normal. It's okay to love an abusive parent but not their behaviour. It's normal to feel a mix of different things at the same time.

Chapter 17

'PARENTAL ALIENATION'; A MINEFIELD YOU MUST BE AWARE OF

'Generally, the term "parental alienation" is used to define the efforts of one parent to prevent the children from having an ongoing relationship with the other parent.'

BE PREPARED

If you find yourself in a high-conflict parenting situation with your ex, parental alienation or accusations of parental alienation can occur. The good news is, if you realise early on that this is happening to your family, you can take some steps to call out and hopefully stop the situation from continuing. You see, the key here is understanding the signs so you can do something about it.

However, it's important to be aware that there is also a risk the term 'parental alienation' can be inappropriately used, and even used against you. Parental alienation is a complex and often misrepresented proposition which has been the backdrop to many studies and enquiries over the years.

Remember the controversial One Nation leader Pauline Hanson? Well, she made a claim that some women lie about domestic abuse to deny fathers access to their kids. Yep, you read that right. And that is not a new idea. Hanson's claim was regurgitating similar comments made as long ago as the 1980s. This claim was one of the drivers behind a parliamentary inquiry into the family law system, which was commenced in September 2019.

WHAT *IS* PARENTAL ALIENATION?

Parental alienation is hard to define and even harder to prove because it's usually based on one parent's opinion against the other. Generally, the term is used to define the efforts of one parent to prevent the children from having an ongoing relationship with the other parent. The thinking is that one parent can manipulate their kids into distancing themselves from the other parent, or even ending their relationship with the other parent. This can happen even if the kids themselves have no reason to stop their relationship with the other parent. They can be coached and taught to alienate the other parent.

Now you may be thinking, *there is no way this is going to happen to my family*. And I truly hope that you are correct in your assumption. But, in my years of working with separated families, and my experience with a fair share of high-conflict cases, alienation can sneak up on you, and before you know it your children are preferring to kick back with some Netflix at their other parent's home rather than joining you on a fun adventure at Luna Park.

Of course, there is also the flipside to this scenario. You know, the part where I say to you, perhaps it is *you* who is dabbling in actions that could, even unintentionally, cause your kids to be alienated from your ex.

I'm sharing this information not to cause you concern but to ensure you are aware, so if you start to think something is amiss with the way your kids are wanting to spend time with their other parent, or you, you can look at ways to get everyone back on track. Alternatively, if you are legitimately concerned about the safety of your kids when they spend time with their other parent and you take steps to limit this contact, you need to be aware the term 'parental alienation' may be levelled at you.

Be prepared.

HOW DO YOU KNOW IF THIS IS HAPPENING?

This is by no means an exhaustive list, but I have included some general scenarios that may point to the occurrence of parental alienation:

- When your ex (or you) regularly interferes with communication between the kids and their other parent.
- When your ex (or you) makes false allegations of abuse against the other and involves the kids in these allegations. (This is a controversial point, and I discuss this more below.)
- When your ex (or you) regularly engineers situations so that the kids are 'unavailable' to spend time with their other parent.
- When your ex (or you) creates an intense fear in the kids of spending time with their other parent, when no previous fear existed.

HOW PARENTAL ALIENATION ACCUSATIONS CAN BE MISUSED

I have been involved in many cases where parents engaged in despicable and irrational behaviour towards each other after separation, and involved their kids. And, sadly, both mums and dads are capable of this behaviour.

Many experts say that a lot of parents who are accused of alienation are mums alleging family violence or child sexual abuse against their ex. In August 2019, research was conducted by the School of Justice at Queensland University of Technology into family law cases that showed parental alienation continues to be raised by dads as a defence to child sexual abuse allegations.

Now just stop for a minute and think about that. If it's correct that some parents are being falsely accused of parental alienation when, in fact, they are desperately trying to protect their kids from abuse, the consequences can be disastrous if the court orders them to visit or live with an abusive parent.

I need to spend a bit of time to unpack this with you. Because if you do believe you are being alienated from your kids, you need to consider whether your ex might genuinely hold concerns for their safety. On the other hand, if you are the parent who is concerned about your kids' safety when they are in the care of your ex, you need to be aware that the term 'parental alienation' may be levelled against you if you try to restrict your kids from seeing your ex.

When parental alienation is raised as an accusation, you can experience intimidation from lots of areas, including from the other parent, Family Report writers, judges and lawyers. These people can paint you as a hysterical, vindictive and manipulative person.

These problems occur in our family law system because the *Family Law Act* promotes equal shared parental responsibility after parents separate. While the term 'parental alienation' isn't included in the *Family Law Act*, a parent who is reluctant to send their kids to the other parent can be seen as being obstructive in the face of 'shared parental responsibility'.

When an accusation against you of alienation gets support and traction from a family consultant or a judge, the kids may be sent to live with the other parent and your access may be severely reduced or totally denied. Although this does not always happen, orders are sometimes made to transfer the kids to an allegedly abusive parent, often even if the kids themselves are making their views clear that they do not want this.

'Parental alienation' first started to appear in cases in the Australian family court system in 1995. Parents who did not willingly send their kids to the other parent were criticised for their 'hostile attitude'. Research then started to find that parents, particularly women, were often not believed in their claims of family violence and child sexual abuse, and their claims were often responded to with allegations of parental alienation.

But, later research suggests that deliberately false allegations of family violence and child sexual abuse are rare. If a parent is concerned about the safety of their kids when they are in the other parent's care, those concerns are usually well founded.

Despite these contradictions, parental alienation is commonly raised as an issue in acrimonious separations, and can be easily misused. This can have dangerous consequences for families.

The moral to this story is to carefully consider your situation and that of your kids, and do your very best to keep their best interests at the forefront of all actions you take.

HELPING TO CHANGE THE COURSE OF ALIENATION

Even though it's difficult to prove and there are many facets to what we know as 'parental alienation', if you believe your ex might be attempting to alienate your children from you, here are 10 tips to help.

1. Tell your kids that you love them always

When you do manage to get time with your kids, regardless of whether it's in person or a Zoom call, tell them you love them and that you think about them all the time. Let your kids know they are special to you.

2. Keep in contact with your kids

Even if you know your birthday cards, letters, gifts, voice messages and emails are being intercepted or not delivered, keep trying. Keep a diary or a journal of your attempts to contact your kids, as well as writing to your kids as if they were going to read it some day in the future. This has the potential to help you and your kids later, if they have the opportunity to find out the truth about being alienated from you.

3. Keep your promises

You know kids like routine, but they like you keeping your promises even more. If you have made special plans with your kids, do everything in your power not to change those plans. Even if you are concerned that your ex will pull the pin on the kids spending time with you as previously arranged or ordered, keep making your plans and stay positive. Expect the best outcome. Always try to be on time and to show up for your kids as planned. If you fall down here, not only does it negatively impact your children, but it can give your ex an opportunity to tell your kids that you don't care, which could further alienate them from you.

4. Just be you

Be yourself and don't change how you feel about your kids. There is no need to be 'extra special' to prove your ex is wrong in whatever they are saying about you. Just be your usual loving, caring, nurturing self. And remember, your actions will always speak louder than your ex's words, particularly as your kids mature.

5. Be rational and reasonable and stay chill

Do your best to manage your emotions. This is particularly important where you have court orders or agreements in place. Do yourself (and your kids) a favour and follow the orders or the agreement and avoid giving your ex any reason to vilify you to the kids more than they already have. Unless of course your kids are at risk – if you find yourself in this situation, get advice from a family lawyer. And of course if there is immediate danger, always call the police.

6. Use positive language with your kids

Try to avoid using negative language when you are with your kids. Sprinkle your discussions with happy, positive words. For example, if you are always saying to your kids, 'I miss you', it can cause them to feel guilty or upset because they are worried about you. Instead, try, 'I can't wait to see you next time'. Another example of using positive language with your children is to try to stop saying things like, 'I wish I could have seen you ....'. This suggests a lost opportunity or a regret. Rather, try, 'Wow, that's great to hear and must have been very exciting'. This statement shows that you are excited and supportive, and you are positively reinforcing the experience your kids have had.

7. Never blame the kids

It can be difficult, but try to remember that your kids are victims when it comes to parental alienation, even if it can seem like they are complicit in it. Herein lies the difficulty. It can often be that if parental alienation is truly happening, your kids may spy on you, talk about your every move to your ex, and report on every purchase you make or who you talk to and spend time with. Please remember this is a part of the alienator's strategy. Try not to let yourself become frustrated with the kids. Don't blame the kids for your ex's behaviour.

8. Put time into building your relationship with your kids

I'm not suggesting that you take on the 'Disney' parent role. However, it can help to make sure your time with your kids, no matter how limited, is quality time. Organising a vacation, going to a game together, reading a book and watching a favourite movie are all examples of special moments you can share with your children to help build and maintain a strong bond and relationship with them.

9. Don't get defensive

No, really – this is one of the most important tips I can give you. If you are experiencing parental alienation, breathe deeply and do your best to combat the natural tendency to act defensively by always explaining yourself to your kids. Worse, you might even think it's a good idea to counter your ex's negative talk about you by saying horrible things about your ex. Don't do this. This is alienation too. Don't fall into that trap of following the natural human tendency to defend yourself against false accusations.

10. Surround yourself with a good support network

Specialist health professionals, therapists and legal professionals are able to assist you with mitigating parental alienation, or accusations of this. Parental alienation can deeply affect kids' emotional and mental wellbeing. This kind of trauma can extend well into adulthood, so it's vital you don't become caught up in the conflict or lose sight of what matters most: your kids. Get help so that your kids' love for both of their parents is respected and encouraged.

A FINAL WORD ON PARENTAL ALIENATION

As I finalise this chapter, I can't help but be reminded of two very distinct cases, one historical case that I heard about through someone who was a victim of parental alienation, and another more recent case in 2019. Both of these examples turn the usual premise of parental alienation on its head. These cases, for me, highlight the very serious nature of parental alienation allegations, but also the impacts and complexity of these situations.

The first case involved a mum who unfortunately was successful in turning her kids against their dad. I say that this was unfortunate because there were no allegations of family violence or abuse made by the mum, but simply that she did not like her ex and went about ensuring her kids severed their relationship with him.

I met with one of the daughters, who at the time was all grown up and in her mid-twenties. She expressed to me her distress and anger at how her mum had been enabled and then supported by the family court to successfully sever her relationship with her dad.

It wasn't until the daughter was older – and she began to properly understand her mum's ongoing manipulative nature and destructive personality – that she was able to properly reconnect with her father. Sadly, but understandably, the daughter now has no relationship with her mum.

In around 2019, I was involved in a case where parental alienation was alleged by the mum against the dad. There were no allegations of sexual assault or abuse against the dad, although the mum had been a victim of family violence at the hands of the dad during their relationship.

The evidence clearly suggested that the dad was systematically alienating the daughter from the mum. What made this case memorable was that, in my experience, it is usually the dad who complains that the mum is alienating the kids. This case was the other way around.

The daughter, who was 13 years old at the time, under pressure from her dad, insisted on living with her dad and spending very limited time with her mum.

The family court did not support the mum's allegations of parental alienation, saying that the daughter was old enough to decide for herself who she wanted to spend time with. Without support from the court, and holding grave concerns for the mental health of her daughter, who was very aware of the court proceedings (which were impacting her considerably), the mum made the very difficult decision to withdraw her court application.

I spoke with the mum shortly after she withdrew her application and she told me she was going to do everything she could to remain in her daughter's life but that she could not continue to put pressure on her daughter to spend more time with her in the face of the dad's iron hold on the daughter. The mum spoke about never giving up on her relationship with her daughter and that she lived in hope that, one day, her daughter would realise what was happening and rekindle their relationship.

* * *

There are no two ways about it. Parental alienation is complex and can be heartbreakingly difficult for kids and parents. Keep yourself informed about what's going on in your kids' lives and how they are feeling about their relationships by keeping those conversations flowing between you.

PART V

CONVERSATIONS YOU DON'T NEED TO HAVE WITH YOUR KIDS

'If in doubt, leave it out.'

SOMETIMES THINGS are better left unsaid. This is especially so if you are going through the splits and you have the care of little humans. A motto that I often rely on is, 'if in doubt, leave it out'. To me, this means that if you aren't sure what to say, or how to say it, take some time to get your thoughts in order before you commit to saying anything.

When you have conversations with your kids about divorce, it pays to be cautious about how much you share and the way you phrase what you do say. While you might feel completely justified to tell it all, the reality is some things are better left unsaid. It's also a good idea to think about the kinds of words and phrases you use in front of your children and what impact they may have.

I've included some important tips in the next two chapters about what you should be leaving out when you talk to your kids about separation. I also take the opportunity to talk about financial issues and the bits and pieces that your kids really should know.

Chapter 18

AVOIDING COMMON COMMUNICATION PITFALLS

'A divorce ends a marriage but it does not end a family.'

THINK BEFORE YOU SPEAK

You may have already worked out that explaining the 'why' of divorce involves striking a delicate balance. While your kids may need a 'reason' for why your family is separating, they also need to be protected from adult information and issues. If you're unsure about what information to share with them, ask yourself:

- What feelings do I have about the divorce or about my ex?
- Do I want to share this information because I need to tell it or because my kids need to hear it?
- How will sharing this information help my kids?
- How might it hurt them?
- Will this information improve my kids' relationship with their other parent or damage it?

THE FIVE-LETTER WORD YOU MUST STOP USING NOW

Have you ever come across a word that just makes you cringe every time you hear it? I have a few, but the word that gets used so often in these circumstances that really worries me is V-I-S-I-T.

Yep, you read that correctly.

I can't tell you how many times I've heard a parent say to me, '...when the kids visited their dad,' or, 'the kids came over and visited me on the weekend'.

This has to stop – right now. Why? Well on the surface it might seem a pretty harmless word. Visiting someone conjures up happy feelings of entertaining guests, having a good time and ensuring our guests are feeling comfortable. Sounds good. In a separated family, what kid wouldn't want to be entertained and have a good time while they're spending time with you? And on the flipside as a parent (who may not have a lot of time with your kids), that time is precious, and of course you would do everything you could to make the time you have with them enjoyable and fun.

But here's the problem: kids and parents are not visitors in each other's lives. They are family.

A divorce ends a marriage but it does not end a family. In fact, your children's needs that they had before the separation are still around after. That includes being connected to and spending time with both parents.

Regardless of how your kids' time is split between you and your co-parent, kids need to know they still share a life with both of you and that they will continue to be a permanent fixture in your lives. But a 'visitation' mindset undermines this. It divides a family instead of unifying it. When words like 'visit' or 'custody' are used, you and your co-parent stop being seen as equals. That's because one parent gets to be the 'real' parent who creates the primary home for the kids, while the other parent becomes just a 'visitor' and is pushed to a backseat position.

A similar issue is when one parent starts to make statements like, 'I let her have the kids overnight'. This puts the other parent in the 'visitor' role and can leave that parent feeling diminished and removed from their kids' lives. What happens next is that tensions between homes can ramp up, and frustration follows.

The 'visitation' mindset also impacts your kids' sense of trust and belonging. When your kids feel like visitors in someone's life, time starts to become very precious. Your kids can start to feel like their relationship with the 'visitor' parent is fleeting and fragile. This can lead to kids being reluctant to rock the boat and they can start to behave in a way that does not reflect their true self. And when kids don't feel secure, it can cause a real problem for the primary parent who, along with shouldering all the responsibility, can also get stuck with all the acting up.

I recall meeting a client a few years ago who was very frustrated because her daughter's behaviour was out of control when she was with her, but when she was at her dad's house she behaved like an angel. The issue was complicated – when my client raised her concerns about the daughter's behaviour with her co-parent, he thought she was making it up and said to her, 'There's nothing wrong with Angie. She's just fine at my house. Maybe you just don't know how to handle her.'

You can see how this scenario could cause a high level of frustration and unnecessary concern for both parents.

You can see how this could impact in the opposite way as well. Just like the dad in my story, when a parent accepts the 'visitor' mentality, kids can start to feel like outsiders in their relationship with that parent. And when this happens, they might start to become detached and feel like it's not worth bothering to be in the relationship. If your co-parent is fanning this flame, it can be easy for them to exploit those feelings and influence kids to reject you.

How can you fix this? Change the way you talk and the words you use. Instead of saying 'visiting with Mum', or, 'Dad's parenting schedule', say 'time with Mum' and 'time with Dad' or even 'your home with me' and 'your home with Dad'.

Help your kids to feel connected and valued in each home, and try to work with your co-parent to ensure kids are comfortable in both. Try to continue acting like a family by providing similar structures and disciplinary techniques and maintain your connection when the kids aren't with you. (See part II for more on this.)

DON'T BLAME YOUR CO-PARENT FOR THINGS NOT WORKING OUT

It can be very polarising when you say something like, 'I don't want to separate but your Mum/Dad refuses to try to fix things'. This sets up your children to blame your ex as the cause of the separation and, subsequently, all the changes your kids are trying to deal with.

You may feel like dropping this bomb, but ask yourself how it helps your kids. The answer is that it doesn't help them at all, even if you believe it's true. It just amplifies their confusion and hurt instead of providing them with support. Put your big-person pants on and look for other ways to support yourself to properly deal with the emotions you might be feeling towards your ex.

DON'T BLAME YOUR CHILDREN FOR THINGS NOT WORKING OUT

I have trouble writing these words because I know we would all like to think we would never actually blame our kids for a separation. But just stop for a minute and ponder this: have you ever caught yourself thinking or even saying to your kids something like, 'If you would just [fill in the blank], your Dad/Mum wouldn't be so upset with me all the time.'

This statement is a form of blame that can create a heavy burden for your kids. No matter what, you know your kids are not responsible for the quality of your relationship with their other parent. It's so important that you take on the responsibility for your relationship with your ex. This will also help you to raise responsible kids, by showing them how you do this in your own life.

Of course, apart from not voicing this to your kids, if you really do believe your relationship broke down due to your children, you should think about talking to a counsellor or psychologist so you can work on mending your relationship with your kids. You are both worth it.

YOUR KID IS NOT A SPY

There have been many, many times clients have shared with me that they have asked their kids to find out about their ex's new relationship, job situation, living arrangements or thoughts about them.

Lean in when you read this because I want it to really have an impact: *your kid is not a spy or your personal secret informant.*

If there is something you need to know, ask your co-parent directly. Asking your kids to take on this role sets them up to betray their other parent. They can feel awkward around you, or even possibly start lying to you out of loyalty to their other parent. It is a lose-lose situation.

At all opportunities, allow your kids to be kids. They love both you and your co-parent, even with all the imperfections that they are aware of.

And remember, if you keep catching yourself obsessing over your ex and their life, take it as a sign that you are still healing. Take steps to invest into rebuilding your own life.

YOU KID IS NOT A CARRIER PIGEON

Newsflash ... your kids are human beings. They are not carrier pigeons to be burdened with messages for your ex.

Do your kids a favour and keep parental communications between you and your co-parent. If you find it difficult to talk over the phone or in person, use email or text messages. There are also some really helpful apps and programs that can help you and your co-parent to keep those lines of communication open. Due to their capacity to synchronise, co-parenting apps and programs can alleviate the need for communication about menial matters. And you may have already experienced that it is often the menial matters that cause the disagreements, which can seriously kill the vibe of your co-parenting harmony.

I've included a list of communication technologies that are designed to help you improve communication and that will, at the same time, keep your kids out of those conversations.

Here are my top five tech recommendations. Some are designed specifically for this circumstance, and some are not.

Our Family Wizard

This platform was created by a divorced couple, and it promotes harmonious communication between co-parents. I think this app is the most extensive co-parenting app available today. Families can share messages, expenses and events. They can schedule and track parenting time and manage the kids' calendars. Families can upload relevant professional contact details like their mediator or therapist. There is even an optional add-on, ToneMeter, that acts like an 'emotional spell check', which can pick up negative tones in your messages and give you alternatives to avoid a potential argument. Helpfully, the app logs communications, which can be useful in providing an accurate record for divorce proceedings.

Coparently

This app offers the tools to make co-parenting easier. With colour-coded calendars, a secure messaging centre, printable records for shared expenses, and a shared online directory, it's worth checking out. You can even add your kids to the account, which can be helpful if your kids are older and need to be involved with communicating about their extracurricular activities. This app offers a free 30-day trial, which gives you some time to explore the app and see if it's a fit for your family.

Cozi

Cozi lets you create shared calendars, shopping lists, to-do lists and meal plans. It has a very user-friendly interface, and the basic program is free. It is one of the simplest apps I have seen, and although not specifically designed for co-parenting, it has everything you and your co-parent would need.

2Houses

This program gives you a way to communicate with your co-parent in an efficient and effective manner. 2Houses allows you to exchange information with your co-parent, such as medical notes and school details, and helps you to stay organised. Other helpful features include messaging with mediator access and document storage. It has an extensive information-sharing feature called 2houses Journal, with the idea that even when your kids are with your co-parent, you'll never feel far away as it allows the sharing of news, photos and videos.

Google Calendar

While it wasn't designed with separated parents in mind, Google Calendar can still help your family stay on top of events and appointments. All you need to do is create a calendar and share it with your co-parent, the kids, and even the grandparents, and give them editing access. It's a simple, easy and free way to coordinate schedules.

DON'T TELL YOUR KIDS YOU FEEL SAD WHEN THEY'RE GONE

You're a good parent and you've learned to put your kids' needs ahead of your own. But it can be easy to forget and slip into an alternate universe during an event as traumatic as a divorce.

Do your very best to stop yourself from telling your kids you are sad or hurt when they are with their other parent. Try your hardest to stop yourself from saying that your kids can't enjoy a special event with their other parent, even if it's not scheduled. These things create conflict for your kids, they often result in animosity between you and your co-parent, and frankly this puts into question your ability to place your kids' best interests over your own.

DON'T USE HOSTILE LANGUAGE ABOUT THEIR OTHER PARENT

Your kids love implicitly, trust, need and value their relationship with your co-parent. Keep this in mind before you use labels, make accusations or use hostile language about their other parent.

The phrase, 'Your Mum/Dad is a [fill in the blank]' is based entirely on your own perception of your ex and is not necessarily the truth. Although it might be *your* truth, this kind of language can seed a very destructive pattern towards parental alienation (see chapter 17).

If you find it difficult to say anything nice about your co-parent, try switching your language to something more positive such as, 'She/he is doing their best at the moment'. By saying this, you affirm that none of us are perfect, but that we are all doing the best we can with what we know.

BE THERE WHEN YOU SAY YOU'LL BE THERE

As you travel through your divorce journey, your kids are going to need constant reassurance from you that they are a valued priority in your life.

If you've already separated, you'll know divorce will totally shift the way you spend time with your kids. This of course can make it seriously challenging to re-prioritise work, family time, and even your personal time.

For your kids' sakes, try to avoid last-minute changes to schedules and organising alternative care arrangements for your kids that can leave them feeling unimportant and even abandoned. Using a system to keep yourself organised is crucial so you can be assured that your family time, work time and personal time all get the required attention. If you find yourself prioritising personal time over the time you spend with your kids, find a way to spend some of your personal time doing fun activities with your children that can be relaxing for you all.

Above all, take up the challenge to keep your commitments to your kids as non-negotiable and the last thing to be cancelled.

Chapter 19

FINANCIAL ISSUES AND WHAT YOUR KIDS REALLY NEED TO KNOW

'Divorce has the ability, more than most other events, to sabotage your future financial plans, and you can find yourself treading water for a while or reprioritising your financial goals.'

Depending on the age and maturity of your kids, it can be helpful to talk to them about financial issues. I don't mean launching into discussions about child support, or whether your ex is supporting you or you are the one assisting your ex. Rather, discussions around budgeting and the reality of your financial situation can assist, especially teens, with understanding why some activities or lifestyle choices can be enjoyed and why others may be off the table.

HOW TO TALK TO YOUR KIDS ABOUT FINANCIAL DIFFICULTIES

Over the course of 2020 and living with a global pandemic, we've learned that almost no family is completely immune from financial difficulties. Jobs can be lost, prices rise, and adjustments are made. Divorce has the ability, more than most other events, to sabotage your future financial plans and you can find yourself treading water for a while or reprioritising your financial goals. And whether you like it or not, your kids are acutely aware of the stress on your face as you work to make ends meet.

You may be reading this and thinking, *Well Bron, I'd rather protect my kids from bad financial news*. But let me say, the tension they pick up on will cause them more anxiety than the news itself.

Don't believe me? Just ask the stressed out 14-year-old who is the only kid in her class whose parent hasn't signed the school excursion note. You know, that note that she asked you to sign last night while you were anxiously bashing out the sums on your iPhone calculator to figure out next week's budget.

I reckon you and your kids are better off if you have some age-appropriate and honest conversations about what's going on, and how your family can work together to get through.

Some conversations you might need to consider having with your kids include the following ...

Talk about changes to spending that might be needed for a time

If you find yourself short on cash, have a conversation about the fact that family holidays may have to be downsized or cut for a while. And spending on extras like fancy clothes, dining out and entertainment may need to be scaled back.

Put your positivity cloak on and present these as solutions to a problem, rather than an unfortunate series of events. Explain to the kids that cooperating as a family with these adjustments is a way they can help the family. Win–win right there.

Let the teens get in on the planning phase

Give your teens an opportunity to see the cost of housing, groceries and other essentials so they can begin to realise how your income needs to be used each month. This will give your kids a realistic sense of the finite value of a dollar, and an appreciation for the money that can be budgeted to be used for the 'extras'. Trust me – this is a lesson that will keep on giving.

Focus on the positives

Some families find that when they have to tighten their belts, an unexpected outcome can be that they start to spend more time together doing simple things like playing at the park, checking out the books at the local library, or having a board game night instead of a trip out to the local Thai restaurant.

Simplicity is a good thing for your family. I know my family experienced much more simplicity when, back in March 2020, we experienced lockdown in Sydney because of COVID-19. We were forced to spend lots and lots of time together. No teenagers racing off to see friends on the other side of town, no excuses to not make it home in time for dinner. And my personal favourite, just hanging out together on the lounge because the dogs couldn't take yet another walk that day.

I say it again. Simplicity is good. Savour it and you may find that your kids learn to do the same.

Assure your kids that it's a team effort

Even if you have to move to a new home or change schools because of financial uncertainty, assure your kids that your family is going to stick together and be okay. What makes you a family is your love for one another, not the stuff you have collected or the place you live in. And that, your kids need to know, won't change no matter what.

IF YOUR EX IS SHARING FINANCIAL INFORMATION WITH THE KIDS

When your ex puts kids in the middle of the big issues, it can be very upsetting. If you find yourself in this situation, you might have already tried to set the record straight and told your kids your side of the story, or kept quiet because you don't want to make a bad situation worse. In the end, neither of these options is helpful to your children.

So, what would be a better approach in this situation?

In my experience working with separated families, sitting down with your children and addressing the issue in a way that helps them process the situation without being involved any further can be a good way to move forward. Now I'm not talking about general budgeting money stuff here. You already know my opinion on this if you didn't skip the first part of this chapter. Depending on their maturity level, kids should be appropriately involved in family budgeting so they can begin to understand and respect the value of money. The issue I am talking about here is when a parent drags the kids into financial disputes following a separation by giving the them a blow-by-blow account of what's going on. You know the drill: mum tells kids that dad isn't paying child support. Dad tells kids that mum's spending the money on herself. Mum retaliates by telling the kids that dad's just emptied out the joint bank account. I call this 'divorce money stuff'. Your kids really don't need to hear about divorce money stuff.

It's okay to tell your kids that you don't agree with your co-parent's choice to share that kind of information with them, and that you're sorry they have been dragged into it. It's imperative for your kids to understand that the grown-up issues between you and your ex have nothing to do with them. Help your kids to know that if the other parent is upset about divorce money stuff or anything else to do with you, it's not the kids' fault, and it's not their job to fix it either.

Make an effort to reinforce that if your co-parent says something that bothers your kids, it's okay to talk about it or ask questions. But sometimes you may choose not to answer a question or to respond to what their other parent has said, because it's something that should only be discussed between the grown-ups.

In the future, if issues about divorce money stuff, or any other areas that are not appropriate to talk about with your kids, come up in conversation, it can be a good idea to ask your kids the following:

- How do you feel about what Mum/Dad said?
- What do you think about that?

These questions will give your kids a chance to think about their own feelings and start to process the situation with you. It can also help you in understanding what's going on for your kids at that time. Remember, communication is key.

If your ex continues to share divorce money stuff with the kids, you could try addressing the issue with them. Let them know you understand that there may be unresolved issues between you both and that you'd really like to shelter the kids from any conflict. It can also take the heat out of the situation to mention to your ex that you value their role in the kids' lives and you don't want their relationship with anybody to be negatively impacted.

TRADING CHILD SUPPORT FOR TIME

Financial survival is usually a major issue in separation. Because of this, you or your ex may be tempted to deny the other parent time with the kids. This can be the case if, say, the other parent is denying you financial support, especially child support.

The *Family Law Act* explicitly separates the issues of child support and parenting time. This is because it recognises the importance of kids spending substantial and significant time with both of their parents (if there is no risk to the child). If you find that you are in a situation where you or your ex is manipulating parenting time in this way, this will demonstrate to your kids the potential dysfunction of your relationship and risks your kids acting in similar ways in their own future relationships. So, stop it. Right now.

There are many ways you can deal with unpaid child support other than using kids as pawns, and your family lawyer can help you explore them.

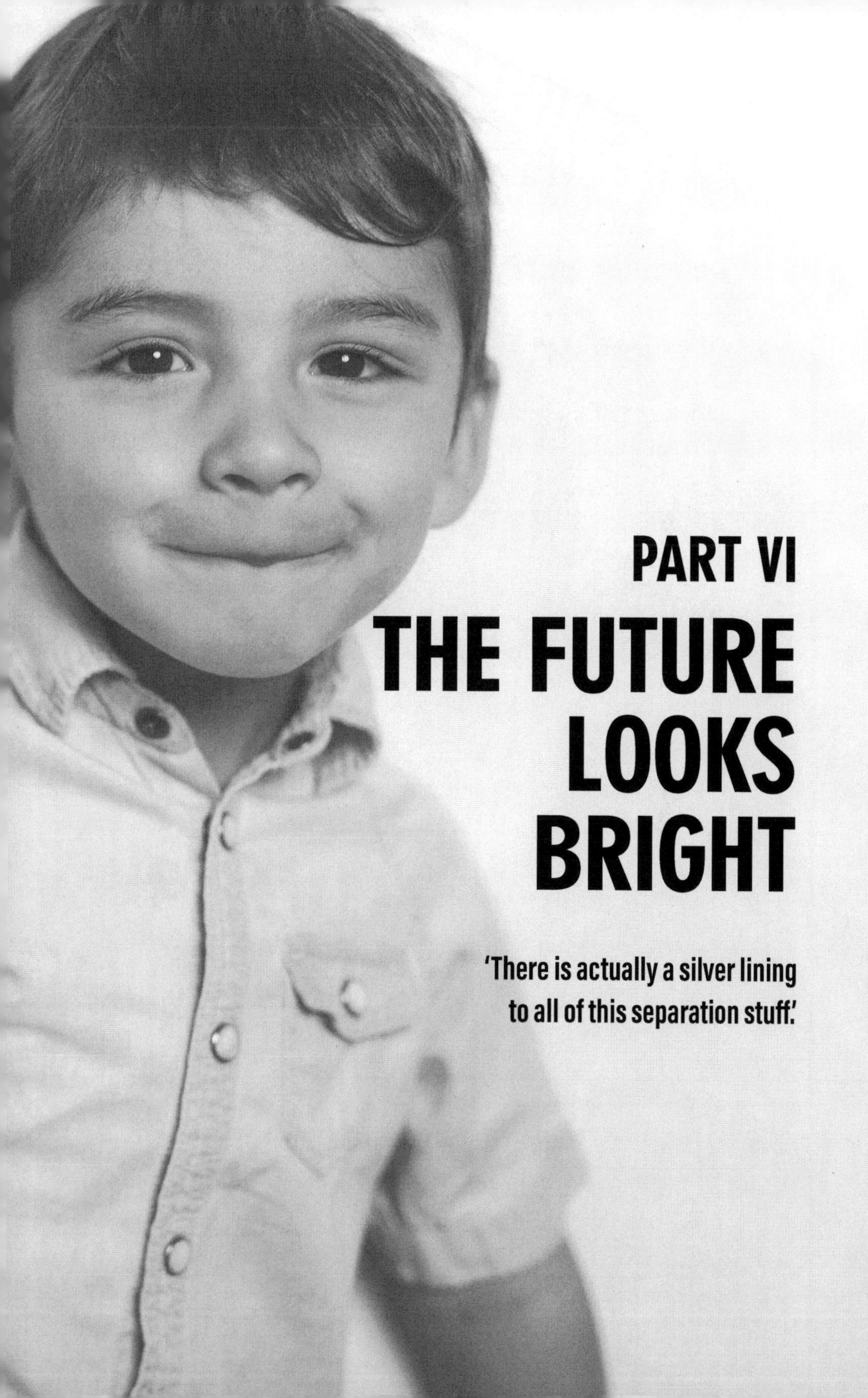

PART VI
THE FUTURE LOOKS BRIGHT

'There is actually a silver lining to all of this separation stuff.'

BELIEVE ME when I say to you, there is actually a silver lining to all of this separation stuff. Whether you have the opportunity to follow an amicable pathway or you find yourself in an adversarial situation, you have the ability and the opportunity to support your kids through the process by talking to them and guiding them. And guess what? For your efforts, your kids will learn resilience. And that my friend is the greatest achievement that will come out of your divorce.

Future proofing your kids is your ticket to a better and more positive life. I want to see you moving onwards and upwards to a place where you can love your life again.

Chapter 20

THE SILVER LINING OF SEPARATION

'I suggest that "resilience" needs to be your new favourite word.'

Divorce isn't the only challenge your kids will face in their lifetime. When children go out into the big wide world they'll have to deal with situations they can't change or ignore. It's a sure bet they will encounter challenges in life that they never expected.

As a parent, you can't protect your kids from every obstacle that life throws at them. But you can help your kids to gain the skills and confidence they'll need to meet these challenges.

When I was researching for this book, I came across lots of opinions about how teaching resilience to kids can be helpful in getting them through the splits. We find ourselves living in a much-changed global community, mainly due to the COVID-19 pandemic, and resilience for our kids is even more pertinent. Throw in a family separation and I suggest that 'resilience' needs to be your new favourite word.

THE SILVER LINING

If you find yourself separating or considering it, here's the silver lining in this very difficult time: you can use this opportunity to teach your kids how to be resilient. Teaching them how to properly deal with change, emotional upheaval, anger, hurt and confusion by being resilient will set them up to be strong and emotionally intelligent humans. And that, my friend, is how we make the world a better place.

In my research I have come across what I understand to be the top six traits of resilience:

1. courage
2. gratitude
3. empathy
4. self-awareness
5. responsibility
6. self-care.

It's important that we look a little more at each of these traits because it will guide and inform you about the best way for you to support your kids through separation, particularly the type of conversations that you should have with them about separation.

You see, one of your top goals throughout this whole process of separation should be to ensure that your little VIPs, your kids, have the opportunity to develop these traits of resilience.

So, let's get to it.

Courage

Sometimes it's the little experiences that can cause stress to kids. When you think of separation, you probably consider that as a pretty big experience that will cause stress for your kids.

If you can encourage your kids to 'have a go' at those smaller activities that cause them stress, firstly with your support and then on their own, it can help them to move past their fears and concerns. By repeating exposure to new things, you can help your kids to build resilience to be able to cope with the bigger things like separation and divorce.

I recently spoke to a client who was the father to 11-year-old Jonathan. My client was concerned that Jonathan was having trouble asking questions of his mum about his homework. We talked about what structures my client could help Jonathan put in place to make it easier to ask for help from his mum. Some ideas we came up with were to do homework when Jonathan's mum was available to answer questions and to use the car trip to school to ask questions. But importantly, Jonathan had to start asking those questions and continue to do so, to help build up his courage.

To help your kids become courageous you should:

- Fill your kids' lives with adventure.
- Let your kids experience, and see you experience, a full range of emotions. Let them become familiar with pain, fear, anger and sadness because this will help your kids to learn to navigate their way through those strong emotions.
- Help your kids to keep going, even if they think they've reached their capacity. But don't push them too far, just gently stretch them.
- Be patient with your kids and allow them to continue to repeat their exposure to new things to give them time to build resilience.
- Tell your kids that you believe in them. Acknowledge their pain or that they are unsure of themselves and remind them of their abilities, strengths and worth.
- Create bubbles of time for your kids to ask you questions. If you don't create those bubbles of time, the questions may not come.
- Teach your kids to know when and how to push back with the truth. If you model truth, it will be easier for your kids to pick up on things that are untrue.
- Share stories with your kids about the times that you stood alone. This will help your kids to see rejection as only a temporary situation and an opportunity to find new special friends.

Gratitude

In 2019, Michelle Mitchell, an author who has written extensively about resilience, expressed gratitude as being 'whatever is in my hands is enough'. I love that quote and the simplicity of it. It's a concept that is shareable with your kids. To teach your kids how to have gratitude, model gratitude. Take the challenge to be grateful for who your children are and not what you want them to be.

And remember, gratitude is contagious. If you are thankful for your children, they are more likely to be thankful for themselves. That is then when the magic happens and resilience grows.

Some ideas to help teach kids gratitude are:

- Teach your kids that there is a difference between real and what they think is ideal. You and I know letting go of an ideal and accepting the real can be really hard, but it's important to be able to do this if we want to enjoy our lives.
- Always think before giving gifts to your kids. You can make it hard for them to be grateful if you give them too much.
- Use bedtimes, meal times, travel times and personal times to inject some gratitude into the daily family schedule. Ask your kids to share what they are grateful for in their day. It's cathartic.
- Take time to notice the small things. Appreciate the way your kids' hair smells, the way they tie their shoelaces, the fact that they remembered to kiss you good morning. These things can be undervalued if we don't stop and take the time to appreciate them with our kids.

Empathy

This trait is my favourite. It can so easily be mixed up with sympathy and I believe that it takes quite a bit of practice to learn how to be properly empathetic.

Empathy allows your kids to see things from another person's perspective and without it, kids won't be able to see things from the perspective of the important people in their lives.

Dr Brené Brown, a social work research professor at the University of Houston, explains the difference between empathy and sympathy like this:

'Empathy fuels connection. Sympathy drives disconnection.'

You see, empathy and sympathy are often grouped together, but they are very, very different. Empathy is a skill that can bring people together and makes people feel included. Sympathy however creates an uneven power dynamic and can lead to more isolation and disconnection. It's actually quite unfortunate that this occurs, when you consider that sympathy usually comes from a good place.

There are four key steps that Dr Brené Brown says help to show empathy. Those are:

1. Perspective taking, or putting yourself in someone else's shoes.
2. Staying out of judgment and listening.
3. Recognising emotion in another person that you may have felt before.
4. Communicating that you can recognise that emotion.

You might be asking yourself right about now, 'Okay. So what? Empathy is a skill that my kids should definitely learn to have, but what's the connection with resilience?'

It's simple. Kids who show more empathy are better connected with others. They are more likely to withstand social trauma well and are more likely to resolve and less likely to escalate social conflict. Sounds good to me to have this trait nailed when your family is going through a separation.

You can help your kids to hone their empathetic skills by following these tips:

- Understand that being 'others orientated' can take some kids longer than others to develop. Accept that it is your kids' default position to think about themselves.

- Help your kids to understand other people have feelings by asking them questions like, 'What do you think your sister is feeling right now about that?'
- Practice and model empathy yourself. You can do this by asking questions instead of making assumptions.
- Teach empathy in family meetings. Structuring some family time to meet and talk can give your younger kids the support to express their feelings to their older brothers or sisters in a constructive and safe way.

Self-awareness

When I was around 12 years of age, I had a very clear understanding of my strengths and my weaknesses. I knew that I flourished when I was around people and that I became lonely if I spent too much time by myself. I felt confident standing up and speaking to groups of people but I struggled to work without praise and acknowledgment. I was beginning to really know myself. I was becoming self-aware.

And this self-awareness helped me to experiment with how I wanted to live my life. The more I experimented and pursued my growing self-awareness, the clearer I became about who I was and what I could contribute.

Kids need their own unique reason to get up in the morning and take those first steps into the day. They need to do and experience things that bring them joy and will motivate them to keep going, even when life gets difficult. This creates resilience.

Some tips that can help your kids to develop self-awareness are:

- Stay flexible about your kids' futures. Although it can be tempting, try not to map out their lives when they are young.
- Give your kids time to play. It refreshes them and is wonderful therapy. They need as much play as possible.
- Be prepared to notice what brings joy to your children. Teach them how to 'Marie Kondo' their lives. (If you have no idea what I am talking about, check out www.konmari.com where Marie Kondo helps people to live a life that sparks joy.)

- Remember that big is found in little. It's easy to reward exceptional talent but often the biggest or most visible talents, like being the smartest or the sportiest, are falsely thought of as the best. Teach your kids that small talents can produce big rewards for them.
- Try to be really careful about what words you use about your kids, especially when they disappoint you. Words can be like sticky post-it notes stuck on your kids' backs that are designed not to fall off.
- Help your kids to work out who their core team is. They need trusted parents and support people in their lives to help them shape their own perceptions of their strengths and weaknesses.
- Don't feed into appearances by placing too much value on how your kids look. As beautiful or handsome as they are, the reality is that they didn't earn their good looks, they were born with them. Sometimes kids who are praised for things they haven't really earned don't always feel legitimately valued.
- Help your kids, especially your pre-teens and teens, to work out who to share personal information with. Kids will benefit from knowing that their best friend will never treat them the same way that you do, and nor can they be expected to.

Responsibility

One day, your kids will not only have to push through difficult times themselves, but they may have to shelter those they love, including your grandchildren. It takes strength of character to accept full responsibility for your time, actions, belongings, feelings and relationships. It's about being accountable.

You may know someone who is unable to move on or get past challenges because they refuse to take responsibility. These kinds of people constantly blame, excuse and justify why things can't be better, rather than being accountable for what is happening. It is impossible to be resilient without being responsible because without responsibility, you become a victim.

Why is it important to teach our kids to be responsible? Kids need to understand that they own their feelings and it is their responsibility to manage and regulate them. You are of course there to help them with this, but ultimately they will need to make choices when you are not around.

Take a moment to consider whether you have ever done the following when it comes to your kids:

- Justified or excused poor behaviour?
- Provided a quick fix to make your kids feel better?
- Done their homework and assignments for them?
- Communicated on their behalf?
- Given them privileges regardless of whether they have earned them?
- Blamed others, including teachers or the school system?
- Done things for your kids that they are capable of doing for themselves?
- Not given your kids significant responsibilities around the home, like feeding a pet?
- Given them money without accountability being associated with it?

This list is not intended to drop you into a pool of self-doubt about your parenting choices. As a parent, I am well and truly guilty of many if not all of the actions on the list. But by thinking about my actions, I find myself coming up with lots of ideas about how I can change the way I give my kids responsibilities that will help them to learn resilience.

And some tips that we could all do with to help kids to be more responsible are:

- Parent with the future in mind and remember the strength of character it takes to be fully responsible at both work and home (which your kids will need to be able to do as they grow older).

- Let your kids learn from real-life experience and remember to be careful not to be so determined to give your kids the best of everything, or the easiest path in life.
- Reinforce with your kids that life is about options and that their choices are very powerful in creating their futures.
- Do your best to stop doing things for your kids that they can legitimately do themselves. For older kids, that includes packing lunches, paying for things, cleaning and doing assignments.
- If possible, connect each important responsibility that you give to your kids to a privilege.
- Perhaps one for the younger kids – try not to give your kids technology every time they are bored. Using creativity is one of your kids' greatest responsibilities in life. It is through creativity that your kids learn to express themselves and interact with others.
- Remember that as parents (and especially mums – I am talking to you), you might tend to over-calculate risk and under-calculate reward. Try this. The next time your kids ask for some autonomy, ask yourself, 'What's the worst that can happen?'
- Refrain from being a 'gap filler' in your kids' lives. You most likely find yourself constantly tempted to fill in all the gaps in your kids' lives so they don't need to stretch themselves by asking for help, solving problems or taking risks. I know it comes from a very good place, but by stepping back, you give your kids confidence that they can do it themselves.

Self-care

When you read the words 'self-care', what do they mean to you? Do you immediately think about pampering at a day spa, making yourself feel better by spending time with good friends, or taking an opportunity to go on a holiday?

You see, it is actually a misconception that self-care is about all of those things. It's actually quite a different concept. Self-care goes deeper than just the peripheral 'feel good' moments. It enables you to be strong, physically, mentally, emotionally and spiritually, so you can give to others.

It can be hard to find the time for self-care, until you realise how important it is to practise it. Some kids naturally know about self-care. They get it. But others really need your assistance to learn how to factor it into their daily lives.

Self-care is the key to helping to enhance your health and wellbeing, manage your stress and maintain your productivity.

Knowing how to self-care is a skill that can take a long time to learn. Heck, I know plenty of adults who still don't get the concept or consider it an important skill to have.

How we all self-care changes with our age. Self-care for a toddler is different to self-care for a teen. And because kids are used to looking externally instead of having the ability to self-reflect, they often use self-care strategies that others use. For example, your teen might look at what reality TV stars do or what their friends do to relax. This might go some way to explaining why so many kids spend their 'down time' wishing they were someone else or somewhere else, instead of truly nurturing themselves and being honest about what fills them with joy.

As your kids move from pre-school to primary school and then on to high school, they experiment with new ways to self-care. It can be hard but it is helpful if you can be somewhat flexible with this but also make suggestions to them when they are struggling to find ways to look after themselves. For tweens and teens, long periods of time being spent in their bedrooms can become normal in their self-discovery and self-care, as well as the frequent wishes to get out and be with their friends.

You can deliberately (and perhaps stealthily) work self-care into your family's daily routine, to help your kids to find their way with this trait. For example, you could set aside some time to exercise together or cook together. In fact, the research indicates that eating together as a family improves grades and psychological health, even when your teen isn't getting along with you.

Brainstorm with your kids and get them to keep a list of the ways that they believe they can self-care. Try these ideas to get started:

1. Have a conversation with someone you love.
2. Read a good book.
3. Get crafty.
4. Take a warm and relaxing bath or shower.
5. Watch funny YouTube videos.
6. Play with your pet.
7. Dance it out.
8. Watch your favourite Netflix show.
9. Put on comfy tracksuit pants.
10. Take off your bra.
11. Write in a journal.
12. Put on perfume or light a scented candle.
13. Get into bed and cuddle your favourite blanket.

Some tips that can help your kids to practise self-care are:

- Teach your kids the real meaning of self-care by getting them to accept they have to take responsibility to be strong mentally, emotionally, physically and spiritually, so that they can be the best person they can be.
- Realise that your kids' self-care strategies will likely be different to your own. And remember that tweens and teens need to experiment with the self-care strategies that work for them.
- Encourage your kids to do something that energises their body every day.
- Technology detoxes are essential if you want your kids to have the opportunity to understand the impact technology has on them. Encourage your kids to unplug for a day, a weekend, or even a week.
- Humans can get addicted to anything that has a reward attached to it. Gaming is all about easy rewards. Help your kids to realise that there are better rewards, and take the time to explore things that give your kids those better rewards.

Chapter 21

10 WAYS TO HELP FUTURE PROOF YOUR KIDS AFTER SEPARATION

'Spend time with your kids.'

After reading this book you may relegate it to your bookshelf or perhaps pass it on to a friend in need. But before you do that - stop!

I want you to find yourself a notebook or a piece of paper that you can laminate, and copy out my top 10 ways to help future proof your kids after separation. The idea is to keep the checklist on hand and in a place where you can check in with it every now and then. Or, if you'd prefer, save it somewhere on your phone so you can pull it out and look at it when you need to.

10 ways to help future proof your kids after separation

1. Spend time with your kids.
2. Speak kindly about their other parent.
3. Don't cry on your kid's shoulder.
4. Work hard to reach agreements with your ex about parenting stuff.
5. Help your kids feel at home.
6. Never put your kids in the middle.
7. Do what you promise to do.
8. Take some time before you date again – but date again.
9. Keep family traditions and routines going.
10. Don't fall into the 'super parent' trap.

Chapter 22

ONWARD

'Heading into the future, you will make mistakes with your kids. After all, you are not a superhero, although your kids probably see you as one.'

THEY'RE GONNA MISS YOU

Of all the changes in your kids' lives after separation, perhaps the most challenging is that one of their parents will no longer be in the next room to help with homework or tuck them in at night. This sense of missing the other parent will no doubt continue for your kids.

Kids feel a sense of connection to both parents, so it's normal for them to miss the parent they're not with. So how can you help your kids to move forward positively when they are experiencing missing each of their parents at different times?

Do your best to respect your kids' love for your co-parent. It's totally understandable if you have mixed feelings about your co-parent at this time. But no matter how you feel about your ex, try to separate those feelings from the needs of your kids. Avoid at all costs the temptation to speak badly about the other parent in front of your kids. You will only hurt their feelings at a time when they need to find a sense of balance and security.

Unless there are court orders to the contrary, or there is a real risk to the safety of your kids, when they want to contact their other parent, let them. You will have happier and more relaxed kids, and your co-parent may just follow your lead.

Allow your kids to settle into their other home. Keep telephone calls short and sweet. Too much contact from you while they are with the other parent can make things harder for them. If your kids are involved in an activity or a meal with your co-parent, get them to return your call when they are free so their time is not interrupted. Your co-parent will appreciate the respect you are showing and may well do the same for you.

Sometimes kids worry about the parent they are not with. They worry that you are missing them or that you will be lonely without them. It can really make a difference to do what you can to ease their concerns. Let your kids know that while you will miss them when they're away from you, you are okay.

> Around two years ago I met a little boy while I was travelling on a plane to a conference in Brisbane. The little boy was travelling with his father to spend time with his paternal grandmother, and he was very excited about the plane trip.
>
> The boy sat next to me on the plane, with his father sitting in the next seat along. He was a very chatty little guy who told me his name was Eric. I guessed that Eric was around five years old. When our snack was offered, Eric was beside himself with excitement and I watched him lean over to his dad and say, 'Can I call Mum to tell her about the cheese and biscuits?'
>
> Eric's dad gently explained that he couldn't call Mum because they were on the plane. Then I witnessed an amazing thing that almost brought me to tears. Eric's dad handed Eric an old blue teddy bear. Clearly it was a much-loved toy. He said to Eric, 'Tell Bear about it.' Eric then turned to me and explained, 'I talk to Bear all the time. When I miss my Mum or Dad, I tell Bear. And when I have something that I want Mum or Dad to know, and they're not with me, I tell Bear. Then Bear helps me to remember what I need to say to them when I see them again.'

Eric's bear was a simple and effective way of reminding Eric that it's okay to miss his parents when he is not with one of them, but that he'll see them again soon.

ALWAYS SHOW UP FOR YOUR KIDS

It's important for kids to have regular and consistent time with each parent. I'm not referring to the length of time here, just that time should be regular and consistent. Depending on the age of your kids, it may not be suitable for them to spend a whole week in your co-parent's care. But even if they are spending two overnights a fortnight, it's helpful to keep that time consistent.

Even if a conflict or strained relationship makes you want to avoid the other parent, try not to let that tension keep you from spending time with your children. And don't keep your kids from the other parent unless you are concerned for their safety or emotional wellbeing. You should speak to your family lawyer before you withhold any time.

Moving forward in your co-parenting relationship, it's an important time to keep your word. When you don't show up for your parenting time, birthday parties or cricket games, you will disappoint your kids and trust can be lost. A promise is a promise. Of course, if there is an unavoidable no-show, apologise and make it up with a special treat or an extra bedtime story. Kids are usually pretty forgiving.

LEARN FROM YOUR MISTAKES

Heading into the future, you will make mistakes with your kids. After all, you are not a superhero, although your kids probably see you as one. Some of those mistakes will include times when you may act in less than skilful ways when you are tired, frustrated or angry. But you can change how you manage things from now.

If you haven't done the best job of shielding your kids from issues between you and your ex so far, take the opportunity to set things right. Apologise to your children and let them know you should have handled things differently. Then, make a commitment not to repeat the behaviour. Give your kids the okay to remind you of your promise if you slip up again in the future.

RESPOND, DON'T REACT, AND BREATHE

Sharing parenting responsibilities doesn't mean you have to be available to your co-parent 24/7. Apart from emergencies, very few situations need an immediate response.

If your co-parent sends you a demanding email or text, or tosses an insult your way, remember you have a choice. While you can't control what your co-parent does or doesn't do, you can minimise the tension for your kids by avoiding knee-jerk reactions when disagreements crop up. Sometimes it takes the old 1–2–3 breathe technique.

Instead of reacting, try the following strategies:

- Prepare. If you need to raise a sensitive issue with your co-parent, spend time thinking through how you can avoid arguing about it or to at least shield the kids from any fallout. Talk to a good friend or a trusted family member to help you to get your thoughts in order, and practise being clear about what you want to say to your co-parent.
- It may help to discuss difficult issues in person at a neutral location, such as a coffee shop. To stay on task, think about writing out the points you want to talk about before meeting with your co-parent.
- Step away. When things get tough, give yourself some time to step back from the situation and weigh up your options before responding. Take time. You could say something like: 'This is an issue we both seem to have a strong opinion about. So, I think we both need to cool down before we talk any further about it.'
- Get another view. It can be hard to solve problems and get perspective when you're angry or frustrated. Go to your support network and speak to someone you can trust to help you sort things out and brainstorm possible solutions.

- Stay focused on the issue and leave your emotions at the door. If your co-parent's communication truly requires a response, then keep it short and to the point. Put your business hat on and don't use emotive language.

LIFE GOES ON

The journey might have started like a rollercoaster, but I am here to tell you that it is possible to get past the extreme ups and downs and begin establishing a new normal for your family.

Kids can find ways to talk about the hard stuff, and also to find some good things about how life has changed. Transitions between homes gradually become smoother as kids learn to cope with their new family life.

Continue to focus on growing resilient, capable, confident and happy kids and it will all be okay. Remember, raising positive, well-adjusted children isn't about being a perfect parent or having the perfect co-parenting relationship. We all make our share of mistakes on the parenting journey.

In some situations, you may be very limited in what you can do to minimise conflict or control the choices your co-parent makes. Try not to let that get you down. Focus on the things you can change and what you can influence. Stay connected to your people and the activities that help you feel good about yourself, and keep finding ways to move forward.

Do yourself a favour and reflect on the following questions to help you make plans for the future:

- Are there things in your life that are better or easier after your divorce?
- In what areas of your life could you use more support to be happier?
- Where can you get the support you need?
- What do you think are the hard parts for your kids?

- What could you do to make life a little easier for them?
- What are some ways you can help your kids feel secure about the love you have for them?
- What are some things you think your kids need to hear from you after your split?
- What do you want life to look like for you and your kids six months from now?
- In a year?
- What does it mean to you to be a family after divorce?

Spend some time having a conversation with your kids about what they have been through and what their dreams are for the future. Here are some questions you could ask your kids:

- How do you make yourself feel better when things get hard?
- What advice would you give your friends about the changes that would happen to their lives if their parents divorced?
- What can we do to feel more like a family?
- What are some of the good changes for our family?
- Are things getting easier for you?

FINAL WORD ...

In my many years of helping families going through separation, I have been struck by the incredible resilience of the kids that I have either met with or read about. They have shown me that moving beyond divorce is possible. While separation is hard, children can still become capable, confident and happy humans.

Although your journey through separation may have started with lots of twists and turns and ups and downs, life has a way of levelling out for most families. Transitions between homes gradually become smoother. Kids find ways to talk about the hard stuff. They also find good things about the many changes in their lives.

Kids will always grow and change. New issues will continue to come up. And you may hit many more bumps in the road. The good news is that getting through the first stages of separation will leave you and your kids better prepared for what follows.

How well our kids do has a lot to do with the choices we make as parents. Raising happy, resilient, well-adjusted and empathetic kids isn't about being a perfect parent or having the perfect co-parenting relationship. All of us make mistakes. And there are times you may be properly limited in what you can do to minimise conflict or to counterbalance the choices that your co-parent has made. The key is to keep doing the best that *you* can. Focus on the things you can change and not the things you can't.

As parents, we can help our kids to grow into delightful humans by reaching out to them, really listening to them, and helping them see a pathway forward so they can begin to talk, process and heal.

RESOURCES FOR YOU AND YOUR KIDS

For more resources for you and your kids, head on over to my website at www.oloanfamilylaw.com.au/helpful-links/

FOR YOU

The Australian Government funds a range of services to help separating or separated couples manage disputes and avoid going to court.

Family Relationship Centres

These centres are a source of information and confidential assistance. Family Relationship Centres focus on helping families to reach workable parenting arrangements outside of court. They also offer services that can help strengthen relationships and deal with relationship difficulties.

www.familyrelationships.gov.au/talk-someone/centres

Family Relationship Advice Line (FRAL)

The FRAL is a national telephone service available to help you with relationship issues. It also provides free advice on parenting arrangements after separation. Callers can be referred to local services, such as Family Relationship Centres, for further assistance. The FRAL is available from 8am to 8pm, Monday to Friday, and 10am to 4pm on Saturday.

1800 050 321 or www.familyrelationships.gov.au/talk-someone/advice-line

Children's contact services

Specialist service providers that provide a venue for you or your ex to spend time with your kids in a secure and supervised environment. See the Australian Children's Contact Services Association website at:

www.accsa.org.au

Department of Human Services (child support)

The Department of Human Services provides helpful information about family assistance payments and child support. You can check your eligibility, calculate child support care and payments using this link:

www.servicesaustralia.gov.au/individuals/topics/online-estimators/28456

Law Societies in Australia

Law Society of New South Wales: www.lawsociety.com.au

Law Institute of Victoria: www.liv.asn.au/

Queensland Law Society: www.qls.com.au/For_the_community

Law Society of South Australia: www.lawsocietysa.asn.au/

Law Society of Western Australia: www.lawsocietywa.asn.au/

Law Society of the Australian Capital Territory: www.actlawsociety.asn.au/

Law Society Northern Territory: lawsocietynt.asn.au/

Law Society of Tasmania: www.lst.org.au/

Legal Aid services

If you are looking to obtain free legal advice, a good place to start is with your local community legal centre. You can find details of your closest community legal centre at:

www.clcs.org.au/

Counselling and support

These organisations can help you with support and counselling services:

Lifeline: www.lifeline.org.au/

Relationships Australia: www.relationships.org.au/

Courts

The following resources provide information about the courts in Australia:

Family Court of Australia: www.familycourt.gov.au

Federal Circuit Court of Australia: www.federalcircuitcourt.gov.au

Commonwealth Courts Portal (this portal is for filing court documents): www.comcourts.gov.au/

FOR YOUR KIDS

The Kids Helpline has a great tagline – 'anytime, any reason'. A great resource for kids who are finding their way through separation or divorce. Call 1800 55 1800.

For younger kids: kidshelpline.com.au/kids

For teens: kidshelpline.com.au/teens

For young adults: kidshelpline.com.au/young-adults

Some helpful books to read with your kids

Max's Divorce Earthquake Rachel Brace
Good for young kids who are living through divorce and are learning how to live between two homes.

Was it the Chocolate Pudding? Sandra Levins and Bryan Langdo
Good for younger kids who might feel anxious or confused by what is happening. Perfect for parents who want to reassure kids that it's not their fault.

My Super Single Mum Bronwen Fallens
Good for parents looking for a read-aloud book that teaches kids to accept all types of families, especially single mum families.

Two Homes Claire Masurel
Good for parents looking for a separation book that is child-focused and easy to understand. Can help kids become more optimistic about their situation.

It's Not The End Of The World Judy Blume
Good for older kids and preteens who are struggling to make sense of their new normal. This book will help them understand that divorce and separation are not the end of the world.

Horse Dreams Mary Vivian Johnson
Good for preteens and teens who love horses and are struggling to cope with divorce and a second marriage.

Candyfloss Jacqueline Wilson
Good for preteens and younger teens who are dealing with the aftermath of separation and the difficulties in maintaining friendships.

The Suitcase Kid Jacqueline Wilson
Good for preteens and younger teens looking for reassurance, comfort and guidance after a split.

The Case of the Scary Divorce Carl Pickhardt
Good for older kids who are struggling to cope with emotions like sadness and anger during a separation or divorce. Good for kids who don't like self-help books but love a great mystery book.

Appendix A

ISSUES THAT CAN BE THE BASIS OF A PARENTING MATTER FILED WITH THE COURT

Please understand that none of the below information constitutes legal advice whatsoever, and you should get legal advice if any of these issues are affecting your family.

Applying to change an existing parenting order

To change an existing court order, you need to be able to show that there has been a significant change of circumstances that makes a change necessary.

If you can agree to the changes, you can apply for consent orders or you can enter into a parenting plan.

If you don't agree, the parent who wants the change to happen can apply to the court with an Initiating Application.

Relocation and travel, including airport watchlist and international travel

Moving with your kids to another state, town or country is called relocation. If your kids live primarily with you, and you need to relocate, you should first try to talk with the other parent.

If you can't agree about relocating, you can apply to the court for orders to allow you to move. The court may not give you permission. The decision will be made based on the best interests and welfare of the kids.

The court has the power to make an order restricting you or your ex from removing your kids from Australia by adding them to the airport watchlist.

Contravention or breach of a current parenting order

When a parenting order is made, you and your ex must comply with it. If your ex isn't complying with an order, you should get legal advice.

If an existing order no longer reflects the current arrangements of the kids, or you or your ex can't reasonably comply with the orders, you can ask the court to vary the existing order.

If the existing order has been breached by your ex, you should try to resolve the issue between you. But if you can't reach agreement, you can apply to the court for assistance.

Recovery and location orders

A recovery order is made if your kid is taken away from you and you are unable to locate them. The court can make an order authorising the Australian Federal Police to find, recover and deliver your kid back to you.

If you believe your kid is in Australia but you don't know where they are, you can apply to the court for a location order. The order then requires your ex to provide information to the court about your kid's location or the Secretary of a Department or an appropriate authority of the Commonwealth (such as Centrelink) can provide information about your kid's location if they hold those records.

Grandparents and carers

The *Family Law Act* acknowledges the importance of kids' relationships with their grandparents and extended family and friends.

If you are a grandparent or any other person with responsibility for the care, welfare and development of kids, you can apply for a parenting order for the kids.

Changing a kid's name

If you wish to change your kid's name, you should firstly try to get consent from their other parent. If you can't get that consent, you can file an application with the court. However, an order from the court alone may not be enough to get a change in the registration of your kid's name.

Proof of parentage

An application for parentage testing can be sought to determine the parentage of a kid. If the court makes this order, the testing must be done through a DNA laboratory that has been accredited by the Attorney General's Department.

The court can issue a declaration of parentage based on conclusive evidence such as the DNA test.

Financial support for a kid who has turned 18 years of age

If your kid turns 18 while they are still at school, and there is a child support assessment in place, you can apply to Child Support to extend the assessment. The extension will continue until the last day of that school year.

Appendix B

WHAT CONSTITUTES FAMILY VIOLENCE?

If you feel that you are experiencing or have experienced any of these situations, make contact with a counsellor or psychologist, or call 1800 RESPECT. Your family lawyer can also help point you in the right direction. Of course, if you ever feel in immediate danger, call the police immediately.

Controlling behaviour

What does it look and feel like?

- Controlling behaviour is when an abusive person gains and maintains power over you.
- It usually starts slowly and isn't always obvious.
- The abuser may try to justify their actions by saying things like, 'I'm just concerned for you', or, 'I care about you too much.'
- Controlling behaviour tends to become more blatant and aggressive over time.
- 82% of women assessed by Safe Steps Family Violence Response Centre, from 2016 to 2017, had experienced controlling behaviours from their partner or perpetrator.

Some examples of the behaviour

- They insist on knowing where you are and who you are with all the time.

- They won't let you go out without them, and if you do, they become angry or they ignore you.
- They won't let you see certain people like friends or family, or they discourage you from seeing them. This is called 'isolating'.
- They call or text you all the time to see where you are or make you prove where you are.
- They go through your text messages or social media to see who you've been talking to and what you've said.
- They tell you what you can or can't wear.
- They stalk you or track you using technology.

Emotional abuse

What does it look and feel like?

- Emotional abuse is any act intended to undermine your self-esteem, to intimidate you or isolate you.
- Emotional abuse can have a significant impact on your self-esteem and sense of self-worth.
- You start believing what the abuser is telling you – that you weren't good enough, or that problems in the relationship were your fault.
- You feel like you are constantly 'walking on eggshells' or you find yourself trying to change yourself or your behaviour to try to make the abuser happy.
- You feel shame, guilt, unworthiness and powerlessness.
- You are experiencing depression, anxiety, emotional instability, substance abuse and suicidal thoughts.
- In some situations, you might become more dependent on your abuser, even defending the abuser's actions to others or denying anything is wrong in the relationship. This is often referred to as 'Stockholm syndrome'.

Some examples of the behaviour

- They put you down all the time or criticise you, call you names, make you feel like you're worthless or that you can't do anything.
- They blame you for problems in the relationship.
- They yell or swear at you.
- They ignore you.
- They make you feel guilty if you don't do what they want.
- They embarrass you in front of other people.
- They threaten to harm or kill themselves so you do what they want.

Psychological abuse

What does it look and feel like?

- Psychological abuse is when someone makes you question your sanity or recollection of reality through manipulation and lying.
- It is often referred to as 'gaslighting' or 'crazy making' behaviour.
- Psychological abuse and emotional abuse can often occur together.
- Long-term psychological abuse can leave you feeling totally unsure of your own sanity and perception of reality.
- You can start thinking that you are not remembering properly or start thinking that you are going crazy.
- It can lead to emotional instability, anger or aggression, due to feeling frustrated at being accused of something you didn't do.
- If you as the victim are misidentified as the abuser by police, counsellors or other support service providers, it can have significant impacts. In extreme cases you may be unfairly served with an intervention order or have access to your kids limited or even removed.

Some examples of the behaviour

- They make you doubt your own recollections or tell you things didn't happen when they did.
- They tell you that you are crazy or have mental health concerns.
- They tell you that you are imagining or over-exaggerating their abusive behaviour.
- They tell other people, including friends, police, doctors, counsellors or their family lawyer, that you are unstable, have mental health problems or substance abuse problems when you don't.
- They tell other people that it is you who is being abusive toward them when you are not, or you are just defending yourself in response to their abusive behaviour.

Financial abuse

What does it look and feel like?

- Also known as economic abuse, financial abuse is when your abuser uses money or finances to gain power and control over you, or unreasonably impacts your financial autonomy.
- You have no or limited access to money, which makes it harder for you to leave the relationship.
- Your abuser knows that by limiting funds, it is difficult for you to obtain rental housing, pay for groceries and schools fees, and that there is a genuine possibility of becoming homeless if you leave the relationship.

Some examples of the behaviour

- They control your access to finances and won't let you access bank accounts or credit cards.
- They expect you to pay bills, groceries and other basic necessities but give you little or no money to cover those costs.

- They 'forbid' you to work or deliberately sabotage your efforts to work, or they refuse to work or contribute to family expenses.
- They take your pay or your Centrelink benefits.
- They take out loans or accrue debts in your name.
- They file false insurance claims or Centrelink benefits in your name.
- They don't include you in significant investment or banking decisions.
- They evade or refuse to pay child support.
- They hide assets from you.

Sexual abuse

What does it look and feel like?

- Sexual abuse is generally widely recognised in our community.
- It is defined as any forced or coerced sexual activity by someone to exert power and control over another person.
- An individual act of sexual abuse is called a sexual assault.
- Abusers are not always strangers and, in fact, assaults are most common between people who know each other.
- 28% of women assessed by Safe Steps Family Violence Response Centre, from 2016 to 2017, reported that they had been sexually assaulted.
- You might experience long-term impacts such as ongoing depression, anxiety, post-traumatic stress disorder, mood swings, nightmares and flashbacks, low self-esteem and physical symptoms like migraines and changes to appetite leading to weight loss or gain.
- You can experience different reactions to sexual abuse. Shock and denial are common initial reactions. But you can also feel guilty, blame yourself for what happened, or try to minimise your experience by telling yourself it wasn't that bad.

Some examples of the behaviour

- Rape – any sexual activity where you have not given your consent.
- They refuse to stop having sex with you if you have asked for it to stop.
- They have had sexual contact when you have been unable to consent, perhaps because you have been drunk or unconscious.
- They have pressured or coerced you into having sex or performing sexual acts.
- They do not use protection when you want them to.
- They deliberately cause unwanted pain during sex, or engage in unwanted rough or violent sexual activity.
- They expose you to pornography when you do not want to be exposed to it.
- They share sexual photos, videos or messages from you without your consent.

It is important to remember that if this has happened to you, it is in no way your fault. The responsibility for sexual abuse lies solely with the abuser.

If you are experiencing sexual abuse ...

- *Ensure you are safe – if you are in immediate danger or have just experienced a sexual assault, before doing anything else you should ensure your safety. Contact the police or emergency services on 000 immediately and try to get to a safe place.*
- *Seek medical help – you may need medical assistance. If you can, go to hospital or to your doctor.*
- *Talk to someone – call 1800 RESPECT.*

Physical abuse

What does it look and feel like?

- Physical abuse is the intentional unwanted use of physical force to cause fear or harm.

- Sometimes physical abuse does not cause an injury or any physical pain, but it's still abusive.
- It can have both immediate and long-term affects on you.
- Immediate physical effects will depend on the severity of the abuse, ranging from bruising to broken bones, internal bleeding, head injuries, permanent disability and even death.
- Non-life-threatening abuse can still have devastating long-term effects on you, such as post-traumatic stress disorder, depression, anxiety, suicidal thoughts, substance abuse, arthritis, migraines and chronic pain.
- 83% of women assessed by Safe Steps Family Violence Response Centre, from 2016 to 2017, had been harmed or threatened with harm. 52% had been choked.

Some examples of the behaviour

- They have pushed, shoved, slapped, scratched, bit or kicked you or pulled your hair.
- They have maimed you in some way.
- They have restrained you, such as pinning you up against a wall or in your bed.
- They have choked, strangled or shaken you.
- They have thrown objects at you.
- They have threatened you with a weapon.
- They have hurt your kids or your pets.
- They have deprived you of sleep or food.
- They have deliberately driven recklessly while you have been in the car with them.

If you are experiencing any of these behaviours now:

- *Ensure you are safe – if you are in immediate danger or have just experienced physical abuse, before doing anything else you should ensure your safety. Contact the police or emergency services on 000 immediately and try to get to a safe place.*

- *Seek medical help – you may need medical assistance. If you can, go to hospital or to your doctor.*
- *Talk to someone – call 1800 RESPECT.*

Technology-facilitated abuse

What does it look and feel like?

- Technology-facilitated abuse is a form of controlling behaviour that involves the use of technology as a means to coerce, stalk or harass you.
- Being constantly harassed or monitored can, like any other form of abuse, leave you feeling powerless and fearful for your safety.
- It can make it harder for you to leave the relationship because you are limited in your ability to talk privately with friends or contact support services that could help you.
- Don't forget that technology-facilitated abuse can and does occur after you leave the relationship. Your abuser can use technology to harass you, abuse you, and monitor and track your location.

Some examples of the behaviour

- They send you abusive texts, emails or messages via social media.
- They make continuous controlling or threatening phone calls.
- They make you prove where you are by insisting you send them photos of your location.
- They check your text messages, social media activity or other internet activity.
- The 'forbid' you to have a phone or limit who you can contact using your phone or the internet.
- The spy on, monitor or stalk you through surveillance devices (like a tracking system in your car or spyware on your computer).
- They share intimate photos of you without your consent (this is sometimes called 'revenge porn').

Work with Bron O'Loan

If you've got great value out of Bron's latest book, there are a number of ways you can get some more Bron in your life.

To find out how, head on over to her website at:

www.bronoloan.com

You can also follow her on Facebook, Instagram and LinkedIn.

Bron O'Loan

If you enjoyed this book and would like to deep dive into learning more about how to help your kids get through separation and divorce, why not sign up for Bron's course?

Designed to arm you with useful information and to support you at the beginning of your separation journey, so that you can confidently help your kids through the separation and divorce process, the course covers the big questions of:

- How can I support my kids going through separation and divorce?
- What should I be talking to them about and what should I be leaving out?
- How does the separation and Court process work and how will my kids be involved in it?
- Why I should be focused on empowering my kids and how to do that through the separation process?

This is an online course that offers practical support and guidance to help you implement the strategies from this book. It's a course that can benefit you and your former partner to help you to prepare and guide your kids through your family separation.

If you would like to know more about doing Bron's course, email **hello@bronoloan.com**.

Would you like to interview Bron O'Loan?

Bron can talk with passion and authority about:

- Helping kids get through the separation and divorce process
- Factors that impact children
- The family law system and its focus on children
- Impacts of separation and divorce on Australian families
- Juggling kids, separation and life

If you would like to interview Bron about any of the above, or her latest book *The Splits: How to help your kids navigate separation and divorce*, please email **hello@bronoloan.com**.

Share your stories with me

If my book has helped you navigate separation and divorce and you've got a story or two to share, I'd love to hear from you. Please drop me an email at **hello@bronoloan.com.**